Street of Dreams

Broadway is both a street of dreams and an interloper of sorts. As envisioned by the Hudson's Bay Company in 1870, it was not meant to be a boulevard or an avenue, but rather a model town. Though the company's plan was never completely realized, over succeeding decades Broadway fuelled the dreams of tens of thousands in different ways.

To a degree Broadway mirrored the growth of a northern city, the expansion of the West and the building of Canada. People passing through Union Station dreamed of better lives in Western Canada or an end to war in Europe. Many settled on Broadway, building homes and careers that encouraged an explosion of growth in Winnipeg. Some, including those who were involved in politics, education or the law, used their time and talents to improve the lives of ordinary citizens. A few built fortunes through a blatant disregard for the law. In one way or another, all left a legacy for Manitobans that can still be seen today along Broadway, Western Canada's oldest boulevard.

Matthew C. Towers / National Archives of Canada / C-041700

Street of Dreams

The Story of Broadway

Western Canada's First Boulevard

By Marjorie Gillies

Heartland

Heartland Publications
Winnipeg, Canada

Printed in Manitoba, Canada

Matthew Towers' lovely watercolor, entitled "The Parliament Buildings at Winnipeg, July 15, 1930", has about it a dreamy Impressionist feel that captures a fleeting moment of pageantry before Broadway, Winnipeg and the rest of the world were plunged into economic and military turmoil.

Copyright © 2001 by Heartland Associates Inc.

All rights reserved. The use of any part of this publication reproduced, transmitted in any form or by any means – electronic, mechanical, photocopying, recording or otherwise – or stored in a retrieval system without the prior written consent of Heartland Associates Inc. (or in the case of photocopying, a licence from the Canadian Reprography Collective, or CANCOPY) is an infringement of the copyright law.

Canadian Cataloguing in Publication Data

Gillies, Marjorie

Street of dreams

Includes bibliographical references
ISBN 1-896150-14-4 (soft cover)
ISBN 1-896150-18-7 (hard cover)

1. Broadway (Winnipeg, Man.)   2. Historic buildings—Manitoba—Winnipeg.   3. Winnipeg (Man.)—Buildings, structures, etc.   4. Winnipeg (Man.)—History.   I. Title.

FC3396.7.G54 2001   971.27'43   C2001-911342-0
F1064.5.W7G54 2001

Heartland Associates Inc.
PO Box 103, RPO Corydon
Winnipeg, MB R3M 3S7

5 4 3 2 1

Credits

Editor
Barbara Huck

Editorial assistance
D. Trevor Anderson, former Dean of Law, University of Manitoba; Paul Côté, Chief Operating Officer, VIA Rail Montreal; Michael Cox, Retired Manager, Manitoba Club; Colette Delaurier, Tour Guide Coordinator, Manitoba Legislative Building; Jean Dorge, Executive Secretary, Government House; Alan Phillips, Manager, Manitoba Club; Catherine Macdonald, Prairie Connections; Lewis Stubbs, University of Manitoba Archives; Michael Woelecke, VIA Rail, Winnipeg; Tim Worth, Dalnavert National Historic Site

Photographic research
Catherine Macdonald

Design
Dawn Huck

Prepress
Image Color 2000, Winnipeg, Canada

Printing
Printcrafters, Winnipeg, Canada

Cover photographs
Frosted elms on Broadway: Dennis Fast
Dome of Union Station: Peter St. John
Union Station, circa 1912: Valentine & Sons / National Archives of Canada / C–148327

Back cover
Street scene: Looking west down Broadway past the entrance of The Princeton Apartments
Provincial Archives of Manitoba / N–10956

Acknowledgements

Few people walk or drive down Broadway today without admiring the graceful elms that arch over the boulevard or noting the impressive early twentieth-century stone buildings scattered among the modern office towers. Yet how many realize that these are the remnants of a time when Broadway was primarily a residential district? And how many recall that just 150 years ago, this was the heart of the Western Canadian fur trade? Other than the crenellated stone gate on Fort Street, just off Broadway, there is little to remind us of that remarkable era.

Fortunately, there are people who know the story of the changes the boulevard has seen over the past century and a half and I've been exceptionally lucky that they were willing to share that information with me as I wrote this book.

First on my list is Heartland Associates, where Barbara Huck endured my computer illiteracy with incredible patience. Without her support and that of Peter St. John, this book, with all its archival work and incredible photography, would never have been completed.

Dawn Huck spent weeks designing page after page of illustrated copy during a summer of extreme heat and historical research consultant Catherine Macdonald mined the Provincial and Medical Archives for suitable, often little-known photos and illustrations.

I had assistance in negotiating the path through the Heritage Grants Program application from Pauline Boulanger and Lorraine Crerie and the staff at Historic Resources Branch, especially Bruce Donaldson and Henry Trachtenburg, who produced pages of data and information about every government building in the city, were enormously helpful. At the Legislative Library, head of services Rick MacLowick and private researcher Randy Rostecki were always ready to assist. And the staff at the Provincial Archives, the Provincial Library and the Legislative Reading Room were all unfailing in their willingness to track down obscure topics.

At the Legislative Building, many people took time to tour me through various departments and later were particularly helpful in guiding our photographers. Of particular assistance were former Deputy Minister of Government Services Hugh Swan, tour guide coordinator Colette Delaurier, building manager Todd Miclash, security manager Tom Bryce, dining room manager Cheryl Friel and Golden Boy reconstruction engineer Michael Hawrylak.

Special thanks are also due to VIA Rail's chief operating officer Paul Côté in Montreal and real estate manager Michael Woeleke in Winnipeg for assistance in writing the story of Union Station. Cultural resource management officer L. Blair Philpott provided information on the station's historic designation.

I will always remember the special tour that Hotel Fort Garry owner Ida Albo and Director of Sales Sherraine Christopherson took me on to show me the spectacular renovations made to the seventh-floor ballrooms, the newly refurbished Macdonald and Provencher banquet rooms and the nostalgic Palm Room off the foyer. Equally memorable was Elaine Belbas' grand tour of the Manitoba Club.

Special recognition should go to the talented photographers whose work greatly enhances the text, especially Dennis Fast and Peter St. John, as well as to Lorne Thompson, whose renderings and reproductions brought century-old documents to life.

Further thanks go to Cindy Scaberas at Heritage Winnipeg and to Murray Peterson and Sheila Grover for information in their historical heritage buildings committee research on Broadway apartment blocks.

I also wish to acknowledge with gratitude the assistance of the Manitoba Heritage Grants Program and its board members for supporting this project.

And finally, I want to thank Val Werier for his gracious introduction, with its memories on a career of reporting on politics and people associated with Broadway and its focus on the elms that he has devoted so many of his columns to saving.

Basking in the sunshine, constructed in a style used throughout the Commonwealth, Government House would be right at home in the Caribbean.

This drawing of Upper Fort Garry in 1871 gives little hint of the dramatic transformation that was about to occur.

Table of Contents

Preface	10
Introduction	12
The Governor's Gate	**14**
Upper Fort Garry	16
A Town called Broadway	**22**
The Once and Future Broadway Bridge	24
The Real Fort Osborne Barracks	**30**
Gathering Place of the Merchant Princes	**34**
Government House	**42**
The Lieutenant Governor	44
The Stately Homes of Broadway	**50**
Dalnavert	52
The Birth of a University	**58**
The Founding Colleges	60
Gateway to the West	**66**
A Plethora of Railways	68
Blueprint for a Fantasy	**74**
Second-floor Spirits	76
Midwife to the CBC	81
Showpiece of a Continent	**82**
Rough Justice	84
The Architects	86
The Golden Boy	90
The Artists	92
The Scandal	98
Palace of Justice	**114**
Land Titles	116
Broadway Today	**122**
Further Reading	**126**

A bird's-eye view rendered in the same year – 1871 – suggests Winnipeg's urban future.

Dedication

To my children Ian, Marsie, Colin and Nancy, and their spouses, and my grandchildren Ainsley, Courtney, Sidney, Marie-Paule, Elisabeth, Claire, Evan and Kayla

In Winnipeg at Christmas
There's lots and lots of snow
Very clean and crisp and hard
And glittering like a Christmas card
Everywhere you go.
Snow upon the housetops,
Snow along the street,
And Queen Victoria in her chair
Has snow upon her snowy hair
And snow upon her feet.

From "In Winnipeg at Christmas Time"
by Rose Fyleman

Winter blankets the Legislative Building and Queen Victoria in her chair.

Dennis Fast

Preface

I've lived in Winnipeg most of my life, but until ten years ago I'd never visited the Manitoba Legislative Building. Then a friend, newly arrived to make a home here, suggested we take a look around inside.

One step into the rotunda and I fell in love with the place: all that light, all that marble, all those towering columns. All those oil paintings of royalty and government leaders, all those mythical gods, and of course, those huge bronze bison.

Later, on a tour of the legislature, I discovered other facets of the building: that the British architect had demanded perfection in the interpretation of his design, that a crooked contractor had defrauded the government of more than a million dollars during the construction process and that some say a ghost occasionally roams the halls.

Since then, I've visited capital buildings in Ottawa, Toronto, Calgary and Victoria to see how they compared to Winnipeg's house of government. I found each city has a legislative building with an impressive, even stately exterior, but they are dark and gloomy inside.

Nor do their grounds equal the Broadway Legislative Grounds, where a scattering of bronze, stone and marble art pieces provide a mix of international heroes and events that reflect the province's ethnic makeup. And none offers that incredible view of our Golden Boy, rushing north into an unknown future.

I knew I wanted to somehow record all this, and when Heartland's publisher, Barbara Huck, suggested I broaden the idea and write about the history of Broadway, another, older Winnipeg surfaced.

It's been a great experience and I hope readers discover a new and different view of a city that is more often unfairly stereotyped for its mosquitoes, potholes and cold winters, than it is for its wonderful scenery, parks, architecture and fascinating people from past to present.

Marjorie Gillies
October 2001

Introduction

by Val Werier

So eager was I to become a journalist that I created my own beat and it included Broadway, a glamorous place indeed to a young reporter.

How exciting it was. I enjoyed going into Union Station, a structure of railway excellence, and the Fort Garry, a hotel of luxury and good taste, as well as our fabulous Legislative Building, set in lovely grounds. We have all these handsome artifacts of history, but I don't think we fully appreciate the beauties of Broadway. They give Winnipeg a sense of continuity and a reason for pride.

The beat on Broadway that eventually won me a berth on *The Winnipeg Tribune* was called "Hotels and Rails". I did this in the evenings (the papers only covered the daytime), so I met the trains and checked the hotels to interview interesting people. I recall the rotund, famous mayor of New York, Fiorello LaGuardia, trying to fit into heavy winter pants for he was off to Churchill.

Agnes Macphail, the first female Member of Parliament, a charming lady, was having a late supper in her room at the Fort Garry, dipping pieces of bread in a bowl of milk while I interviewed her.

Travellers got much better service than they do today when they stayed at railway hotels. No waiting at airport carrousels or facing the prospect of missing luggage. It was transported from the train onto carts, then pushed onto Broadway by porters to the Hotel Fort Garry and on to your room.

Broadway was always in the news, for here resides the seat of power, the Legislative Building. I have seen all the provincial capitals (save Nunavut and the Northwest Territories) and I regard the one on Broadway as the finest of them all in its space, appointments and architecture: a veritable museum of elegance. I covered the legislature at one time and learned of pomp and pomposity and bureaucracy – and that underneath it all we are all quite ordinary people.

There was a minister of limited understanding but verbose of speech trying to cope with a barrage of questions from the Opposition. He was completely lost, mouthing words that said nothing. I could hear his colleague,

Attorney General J.O. McLenaghen, advise him repeatedly in a stage whisper: "Read the Act." This he earnestly did, reciting the deadly prose of the proposed law, replete with "whereas" and "wherefore" while Mr. McLenaghen, engulfed in laughter, kept inciting his unfortunate colleague. This was farce at its best.

The Manitoba Club, neighboring the Hotel Fort Garry, was once a seat of power, too. It was *de rigeur* for publishers and editors to be members of this "Old Boys Club", which wielded great influence in government and finance. This era ended with the election of Ed Schreyer and his NDP government in 1969 – the first so-called socialist government in Manitoba.

I also covered the Law Courts, another building of splendor with its marble floors, oak panelling and high vaulted ceilings with stained glass. Here I reported on one of the most dramatic stories of my career. A man in his late seventies, a widower jilted by his lady friend, went berserk and killed her with an axe. At his trial, this man of Russian origin could not understand the official interpreter and asked his son to translate when the judge pronounced sentence. He had to tell his father: "You will be hanged by the neck until you are dead." The penalty was not imposed, however, because the man was considered insane.

Looking east down Broadway in mid-summer.

Broadway has a distinction shared by few such precincts, and Marjorie Gillies, a veteran journalist, has presented us with many fascinating stories to illuminate the splendor of its historical buildings.

They are of national fame with their facades of our native Tyndall stone displaying the outline of fossils deposited millions of years ago. It is notable that Tyndall stone has been used in the House of Commons in Ottawa and many other prominent buildings in Canada.

Broadway is beautiful because of its elms, planted at the turn of the century and today a bower of magnificence. It is incomprehensible that merchants once wanted the centre boulevard removed of trees for parking.

Broadway is a people place mainly because of the environment created by the trees. We should be vigilant about protecting our Broadway. A gasoline station at Broadway and Main Street obscures the Fort Garry Gate Park, a place of deep historical significance. It's something we should never have allowed to happen.

Broadway tells us something more: it pays to construct public buildings in a grand manner.

The Governor's Gate

A pair of coureurs du bois *stop for a pipe with their dogs at the old Fort Garry Gate in 1904.*

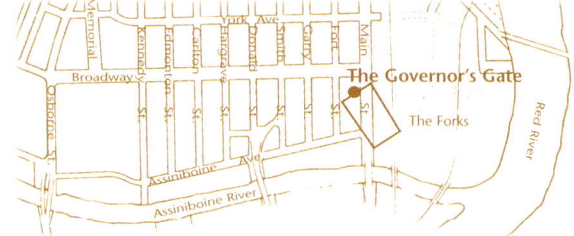

The last remnant of what was once the heart of the fur trade has quite handily survived the ravages of time, but was nearly destroyed – not once but several times – by the plunderings of progress. The gate's history is one of rejection and threatened destruction and its existence today, as the centrepiece of Fort Garry Gateway Park on the east side of Fort Street, seems due more to luck and happenstance than civic planning.

The last remnant of Upper Fort Garry, which was dismantled in 1881–82, the gate is a shell structure. The only decoration on its bare stone walls are commemorative plaques placed by the Canadian Club of Winnipeg and the Historic Sites Advisory Board of Canada. There is also a plaque to Ambroise-Didyme Lépine, Louis Riel's adjutant

The Governor's Gate

general. The gate stood at the rear entry to the fort, in the north wall; the front entry faced the Assiniboine River. It was built when Upper Fort Garry was expanded in 1853 by Alexander Hunter Murray, a journalist, artist and journeyman builder who joined the Hudson's Bay Company in 1846 to build Fort Yukon. He designed the stone gate at Upper Fort Garry when the property was expanded to make room for a home for the HBC governor.

The stonework was done by laborers recruited from the Chelsea Pensioners regiment, who had come from England to attempt to defend the HBC's monopolist trade policies. **TO PAGE 18**

Government House, the home of governors of Rupert's Land and later of Manitoba's lieutenant governors, rises behind the Governor's Gate in this 1879 winter scene by Lionel MacDonald Stephenson.

Lionel MacDonald Stephenson / National Archives of Canada C-2042314

Upper Fort Garry

The Governor's Gate is but a small reminder of the formidable fort that once dominated the confluence of the Red and Assiniboine Rivers. With four large bastions and five-metre-high walls, it was a visual demonstration of the Hudson's Bay Company's commanding role in the fur trade. Built in 1835 and named Upper Fort Garry to distinguish it from Lower Fort Garry built four years earlier, it was the second so-named fort built near the strategic junction of the Red and Assiniboine Rivers, and the last of four forts that rose and fell within a century of the coming of Europeans to the region. The first was Fort Rouge, established in 1738 for Pierre Gaultier de la Vérendrye, was one of a network of trading posts from Lake Superior to Lake Winnipeg. The timbers of this fort are said to lie beneath the junction of Winnipeg's two major thoroughfares, Portage Avenue and Main Street, but no visual evidence of the structure lingers. La Vérendrye's forts were built with haste and Fort Rouge was likely a crude wooden structure, a European oddity on the boundless prairie, and destined to deteriorate. The name lingers today only in the name of Winnipeg's first suburb – Fort Rouge – that stretches southwest of the forks of the Red and Assiniboine.

It was not until the turn of the nineteenth century, when rivalry between the HBC and the North West Company intensi-

Henry James Warre's rather whimsical 1845 depiction of Upper Fort Garry recalls a medieval European castle.

fied in Red River, that fort building at The Forks began in earnest. In 1806, the Nor'Westers built Fort Gibraltar within fifty metres of the Red River's west bank in opposition to the HBC, and, within a few years, to buttress the attack on the Scottish settlers brought in by the HBC's majority share holder, Thomas Douglas, Earl of Selkirk. Its stockade made of oak trees split in two, its picketing as high as five metres, Fort Gibraltar shielded eight houses within its walls and lasted until March 1816 when HBC officers and men seized and destroyed it.

To stake its claim in Red River, the HBC had built Fort Douglas nearby in 1813, and with the destruction of Fort Gibraltar the company seized control of the Red and denied passage and provisions to the Nor'Westers. In June 1816, some Nor'Westers and their allies captured Fort Douglas after killing the local HBC governor and twenty of his men at Seven Oaks, a few kilometres north of the fort.

Lord Selkirk restored order with the help of disbanded Swiss mercenary soldiers and the Nor'Westers rebuilt Fort Gibraltar. But in 1821, after an epic struggle, the two fur trading companies merged and Fort Gibraltar, better situated at The Forks, was taken over by the HBC and renamed Fort Garry. Fort Douglas was sold to a Red River settler in 1825 and vanished the following year in one of the most severe floods in the Red River Valley's recorded history.

The 1826 flood so damaged Fort Garry that the HBC constructed a new post, Lower Fort Garry, thirty-two kilometres north along the river, as its administrative centre. But by 1836, with the Red River colony clearly settled and growing at the junction of the Red and Assiniboine, the HBC returned to The Forks and built a new fort, Upper Fort Garry, an impressive structure with barracks, officers quarters, chief factor's residence, general store, fur store, pemmican store and governor's residence.

By 1870, the fort was a more business-like place that served a growing multicultural community, including traditional customers like Mild Elk Spirit (inset) and the first of what would soon be a flood of immigrant settlers.

In the early 1850s, with trade increasing, the fort was extended to the north with the Governor's Gate as a private entrance to the governor's house and gardens. The fort remained the seat of government for the District of Assiniboia and the Red River settlement until 1870 when the Province of Manitoba was created.

Street of Dreams: The Story of Broadway

This map shows the community at The Forks in 1872. Broadway, as yet unnamed, heads west behind Fort Garry, "Main Road" leads to the Assiniboine River, while a trail leads to the Red River and the ferry to St. Boniface. The ferry was still transporting passengers in 1881, when this painting was created.

Constructed of a combination of cut limestone blocks and limestone rubble, it has a large central arch, gun portals, a bastion for a guard house and a crenellated top. It's believed to contain remnants of the North West Company's Fort Gibraltar, which was rebuilt in 1821 when that fur trading company amalgamated with the Hudson's Bay Company.

Fort Gibraltar was soon renamed Fort Garry after Deputy-Governor Nicholas Garry, who had overseen the union of the two companies.

By the spring of 1882, only four small buildings, the Governor's House and the gate remained on the fort site. The buildings were sold for $292 and the house for $100 and a future as firewood. The gate's prospects were uncertain at best. Over the next seventy years, it was rejected as a gift to the city; almost torn down and rebuilt on another site, not just once, but twice, and nearly razed and replaced by a clubhouse. On two occasions, in 1912 and again in 1962, it almost became the main attraction in a civic park in downtown Winnipeg. The latter plan was also to contain the 1897 Queen Victoria Jubilee fountain, which had stood at the site of the old City Hall on Main Street. With the old building about to be replaced, a new home was being sought for the fountain.

In the intervening decades, Canadian, British and American souvenir hunters carted off thousands of stone chips in a preview of the fall of the Berlin Wall at the end of the twentieth century. And visitors by the tens of thousands had their photographs taken beside the old gate. Among them were Buffalo Bill Cody and his enormously popular troup of performers, on a tour of Winnipeg in 1910.

Somehow, through luck or circumstance, the structure survived all these assaults.

In 1886, the gate was offered, free of charge, to the Winnipeg government by Charles J. Brydges, the HBC land commissioner, on condition that it be dismantled and re-erected elsewhere. With admirable foresight, City Council preferred to preserve the gate where it stood and attempted to buy ten lots around it. But the deal fell through when council members felt the $8,000 asking price for the lots was too much.

Map: The Winnipeg Free Press
Painting: Frederick B. Schell / National Archives of Canada / C-120519

Renewed and refurbished, the Governor's Gate is a hidden treasure that continues to draw thousands of visitors in search of the past.

The Manitoba Historical Society stepped in next, asking both the Hudson's Bay Company and HBC Governor Donald Smith for a donation of the site or its sale at a nominal figure.

As the gate grew more and more dilapidated and proposals were made to build an athletic field on the property in 1893, the Historical Society scaled down its request to include just the two lot sites on which the gate was located. The HBC responded with a quote of $2,400 for the lots, but public contributions to save the gate were not forthcoming.

Once again, a suggestion was made to move the structure across Main Street

Four years later, in 1897, the Winnipeg Athletic Organization proposed a clubhouse and gymnasium to be built on the east side of Fort Street south of Broadway, close to the gate site. Then unexpectedly in 1900, the HBC gave the "tottering" structure and four of the reserve lots to the City of Winnipeg "as a public park forever". According to subsequent media reports, quick work on its tumbledown condition soon restored the gate to its former "noble and warlike aspect".

Still, controversy continued, this time over the choice of a name. There were protests against calling it the Strathcona Gate, which echoed one

Though maintained for the next fifty years by the Public Parks Board, by the 1940s, the gate was in poor condition. It had survived the predations of lacrosse, hockey and toboggan teams playing on empty land nearby and had almost fallen into the ignominy of becoming part of a miniature replica of the old fort in an extended park

Then, to the surprise of city workers in 1943, it was discovered that both the outer and inner gates had disappeared. Both have since been replaced.

By 1960, the park had become overgrown and was all but invisible from the street, surrounded as it was by a gas station, the Manitoba Club

and rebuild it as the entrance to a new athletic park. But when the dust settled, again the gate stayed in the place in which it had been built in the 1850s.

of Donald Smith's titles. The public wanted no ties to the monopolistic HBC powers. Eventually, the name Fort Garry Park won the day.

and the Grain Exchange Curling Club. A plan for a larger park, to include the statue and fountain of Queen Victoria mentioned above, was never completed

The Governor's Gate

but the vines were removed from the gates, seven trees were cut down and new flower beds were planted.

Twenty years later, under the federal Agreements for Recreation and Conservation (ARC) Program, the gateway was restored as part of a multi-million dollar revitalization of The Forks, the historic confluence of the Red and Assiniboine Rivers.

The $160,000 facelift included removing fill from around the gate, erecting fifty-nine metres of replica wood fencing to simulate the 1850s wooden wall and placing a mural inside the gate, providing an approximate view through the gate of the scene in 1881. During this restoration work, it was discovered that a nineteenth-century bronze cannon had gone missing. It has never been recovered.

Today the large mural – actually an enlarged nineteenth-century photo of the governor's house and garden just before the fort was torn down – is still visible as one enters the gate. This same photograph can be seen on page 43, in the chapter on Government House.

Unfortunately, the mural has been vandalized and graffiti, most of it people's names in chalk, can be seen on the wooden walls.

Still, a walk though the park and the gate's guard house leaves a haunting sense of having stepped back through time, to an era when voyageurs travelled the rivers, and Upper Fort Garry was the center of the fur trade world.

This series of photographs, from far left, shows how remarkably little the old gate has changed since 1876, when Lt. Gov. Morris posed with his eldest daughter. In 1880, Lt. Gov. Joseph Edouard Cauchon was the last occupant of the house. The gate stood alone in 1895, when a traveller in his cariole stopped with his dogs; fifteen years later, when Buffalo Bill (in right front, wearing a black hat) and his troupe stopped for a photo op, ivy had covered the walls. The trees were reaching a fair size when the next photograph was taken in 1925 and, by 1960, all but hid the gate from view. Both vines and trees were removed in a '60s overhaul, as can be seen in the final photograph.

Left to right: National Archives of Canada / PA–28581; F.V. Bingham / National Archives of Canada/ PA–127359; Albertype Co. / National Archives of Canada / PA–31537; Provincial Archives of Manitoba / N10773; John Boyd Collection / National Archives of Canada / PA–87214; Albertype Co. Collection / National Archives of Canada / PA–31589.

A Town called Broadway

Peter St. John

Period lamp posts recall Broadway's Victorian beginnings.

To stroll down Broadway, jewel of Winnipeg's street system, is to witness decades of Canadian history, beginning when the Hudson's Bay Company transferred its vast territories to the Dominion of Canada in 1869, allowing Manitoba to enter Confederation.

It's both a street of dreams and an interloper of sorts. As envisioned by the HBC, Broadway was not meant to be a boulevard or an avenue, but rather a model town, an upscale community where well-to-do families could live apart from the dust and noise of the hectic building boom that was occurring farther north as the pioneer village of Winnipeg exploded into a rowdy thriving metropolis. The town of Broadway, all but forgotten today, was conceived when the newly confederated Canadian government agreed to allow the 200-year-old

A Town Called Broadway

HBC to retain a 500-acre (200-hectare) property adjacent to its fur trading post at Upper Fort Garry, at the forks of the Red and Assiniboine Rivers. (Additional tracts of 500 acres of land adjacent to Lower Fort Garry and White Horse Plains were also allocated by the Dominion Government to the HBC.)

At the same time, a fifty-acre (twenty-hectare) parcel of land abutting today's Osborne Street was reserved by the Canadian government for future construction of public buildings by the new Province of Manitoba.

Bisecting this model town, the first wide European-style boulevard in Western Canada can be clearly seen in

TO PAGE 26

Viewed from the site of the breweries and brothels on the southwest corner of Broadway and Osborne (occupied today by Great West Life), All Saints Church is edged by fields in this 1894 watercolor. To the right of it are the original Manitoba Courthouse with its clock tower and the square tower of the Fort Osborne Barracks drill hall. After 1901, when the University of Manitoba was built just west of the courthouse, this was humorously known as the Four Corners – representing Education, Legislation, Damnation and Salvation.

F.F. Dixon / Provincial Archives of Manitoba/ B1/4

23

The Once and Future Broadway Bridge

For centuries, even millennia, the Red and Assiniboine Rivers served as highways, supply routes and connectors, bringing water-borne people together in the summer, creating trails of ice in the winter, providing food and community year round. For a time after Europeans began to settle in large numbers around the confluence of the rivers, ferries joined the canoes and York boats on the water. But by the time Winnipeg became a city in 1873, its citizens had begun to turn their backs on the rivers in favor of roads and soon, rails.

By the early 1880s, the rivers had become barriers, separating – rather than joining – the older francophone community on the east side of the Red and its rapidly growing anglophone neighbor on the west. The answer, the citizens of both communities decided, was a bridge. In fact, Winnipeggers were on a bridge building

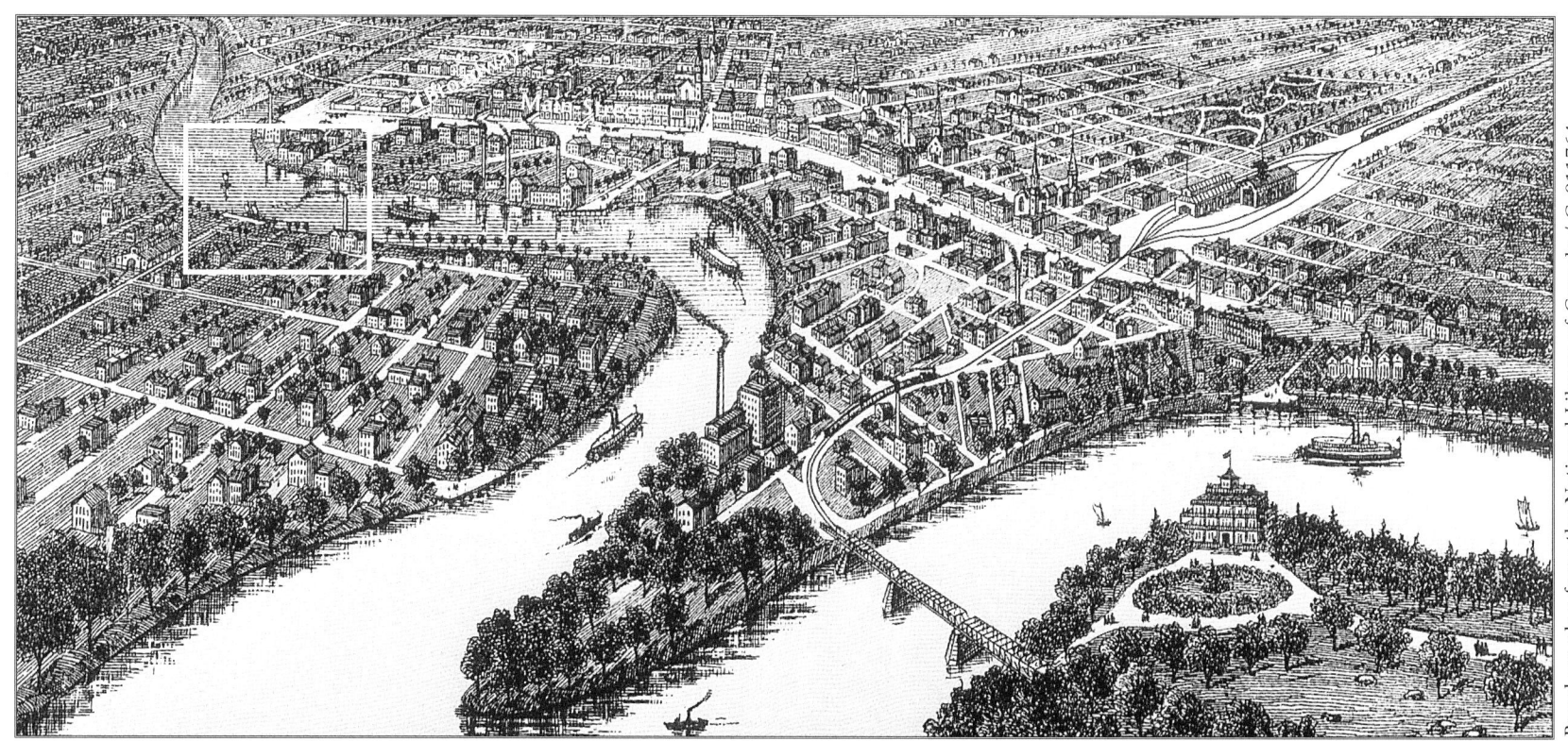

The exploding growth of the city is clearly visible in this remarkable woodcut, a birds-eye view of Winnipeg in 1882. The spanking new Louise Bridge dominates the foreground, while the white box in the upper left marks the location of the first two Broadway Bridges.

spree. Inspired by the construction of the Louise Bridge over the Red River, which was funded by the City of Winnipeg for the Canadian Pacific Railway, a total of five bridges were built between 1881 and 1883. Two of these were Broadway Bridges (the others were the first Main Street Bridge, constructed privately in 1881 and purchased by the city the following year, and the first Osborne Street Bridge, built in 1882; both spanned the relatively docile Assiniboine River). The Broadway Bridges crossed the wider, more powerful Red. Just how powerful, the bridge builders quickly learned. The first incarnation was built during the winter of 1881-82 and opened with a certain fanfare in April 1882. Just four days later, however, the new bridge was swept away by rampaging ice during the annual spring breakup.

The second version was apparently more sturdily built, for it lasted nearly thirty-five years, and served the citizens of both communities for three decades. Both Broadway Bridges followed the axis that leads east from Broadway, through the land that is now The Forks, directly over the Red River to Provencher Boulevard.

After 1883, Winnipeg exploded in size and vehicular and streetcar traffic over the Broadway Bridge increased annually. By 1910, there were concerns about its safety. Still, when it was closed in 1912 following the construction of Union Station, there was an outcry, particularly from St. Boniface. Citizens felt "humiliated" that their direct access to Winnipeg had been so summarily ended.

"Since the regrettable closure of Broadway, we are forced to make a diagonal detour to access the streets of Winnipeg," one wrote, adding, "this bridge is now no more than an ugly heap of scrap-metal that groans in the wind."

The answer, quite obviously, was to build a replacement, and as quickly as possible. The Provencher Bridge, which angles northwest from Provencher to Water Avenue, opened in 1917 and still serves the city today.

But for some, the dream of a bridge once again linking Broadway and Provencher, a bridge for pedestrians as well as for vehicles, never really died. And now, nearly 125 years after the first Broadway Bridge opened, the third incarnation of this historic link is about to become reality.

Beginning with a public consultation process in 1999 and moving through the development of designs in 2000 and 2001, a "paired bridges alternative", featuring a five-metre wide pedestrian bridge (following the original Broadway axis) and a multi-lane vehicular bridge (to replace the Provencher Bridge), has been adopted by the city council.

The pedestrian link, a cable-stayed bridge with a forty-metre tower and mid-stream meeting space, will likely be the showpiece of the project. Connected by walkways through The Forks and Union Station, it will at long last allow the kind of communication between communities and cultures envisioned so long ago by the urban planner who laid out the original axes of the City of Winnipeg.

The Paired Bridges Solution

Street of Dreams: The Story of Broadway

an 1874 survey sketch. The four-lane avenue required nearly three-and-a-half acres (or 1.4 hectares) over its course from Main Street to Colony Creek (today's Osborne Street).

To attract well-to-do families to its model town, the Hudson's Bay Company designed its 500 acres with grid-style streets running parallel, north to Portage Avenue (the original Portage Trail of the fur trade), east to Main Street (the old Pembina Trail to Upper Fort Garry); south to the Assiniboine River and west to Kennedy Street where the land reserved by the government began.

The lots were to be 120 by fifty feet (or thirty-six by fifteen metres) in size, with broad streets and back lanes, providing space to build mansions surrounded by yards where children could play. This proposed street plan was far removed from the traditional HBC lot patterns, where land grants made to retired company servants (as employees were called) ran in narrow strips back from the Red or Assiniboine Rivers. All residential lots were to be sold only to builders, not to speculators, to guarantee housing permanence in the district. Trees were planted along "the Broadway" as soon as the centre boulevard was completed.

In the 1870s, the company envisioned that the hub of business would develop north and south of Upper Fort Garry, the historical centre of transportation, trade and business for a vast part of North America. The HBC reserve housing lots, though promoted at inflated prices, were seen as an accessible choice for the wealthy professionals and fortune hunters already arriving in Canada's "last frontier".

At the time of its land transfer, and even with Winnipeg's incorporation as

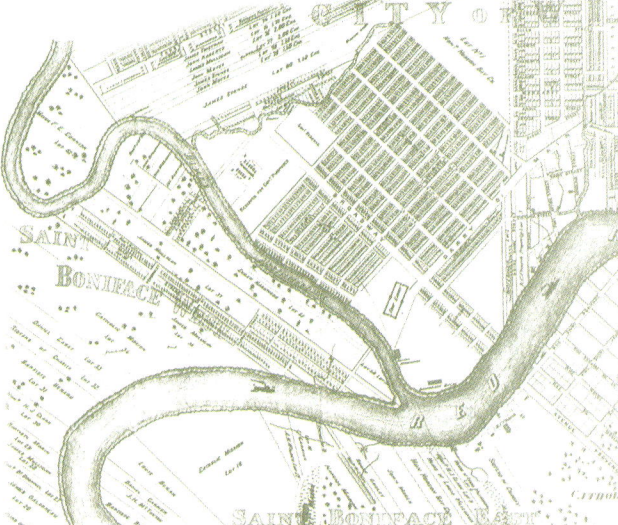

Created a year after Winnipeg was incorporated, this 1874 plan clearly shows the HBC Reserve, with Broadway bisecting it, northwest of The Forks. It also demonstrates the city's early optimism, for the subdivisions shown are mainly dreams. As seen from Union Station, today's Broadway is a mix of past, present, and increasingly, future.

John D. Parr / National Archives of Canada / NMC-23816

Dennis Fast

By 1910, Broadway's early promise was fast being realized. Viewed from Main Street, the slender elm saplings had become sizeable trees and streetcars linked one end of the boulevard with the other. Overlooking the street, the Manitoba Club (at left) and the Strathcona, one the city's loveliest apartments, preceded the construction of two of Broadway's most recognizable landmarks – Union Station and the Fort Garry Hotel.

Broadway Avenue, Winnipeg Man.

Street of Dreams: The Story of Broadway

> Soon, "iron workers", as they were called, were hanging high above Broadway as the Hotel Fort Garry went up.

a city in 1873, the company still anticipated the transcontinental railway, soon to link the country from coast to coast, would travel east and west from its forks property, further ensuring the growth of a business center edging its land reserve. But company expectations went awry when it switched from its traditional interest in the fur trade to speculation and land development.

In 1873, the commercial dynamics of the region changed almost in the blink of an eye. As its population soared, independent businessmen who had already distanced themselves from Upper Fort Garry by locating their shops and offices near Portage and Main became determined to avoid a return to an HBC monopoly.

The newly elected City Council quickly joined all land holdings adjacent to the HBC reserve under one system of laws and regulations aimed at authorizing the passage of public works bills for the construction of sewer and water lines, streets and sidewalks, and the creation of a police force and fire brigade.

Looking to the future, the city fathers next agreed to contribute $300,000 towards the cost of building the Louise Bridge across the Red River, and provide tax free land in perpetuity at Main Street and Higgins Avenue for the rail yards. It kicked in a further $200,000 toward the cost of the rail yards and another $300,000 for a passenger station to provide the Canadian Pacific Railway mainline with ready entry at Point Douglas, not The Forks.

Unwilling to accept the idea that Point Douglas might be chosen as the yard and station site, rather than its 500 acres, the HBC decided in 1880 to demolish its stone fortress at the confluence of the rivers. Walls and corner bastions, the stores, storage facilities, offices and barracks were all cleared away to remove any barrier a rail mainline might encounter.

Removal of the fort allowed the straightening of south Main Street and the construction of a bridge across the Red River to St. Boniface, a tangible link between the French and English-speaking communities. But the CPR had chosen Point Douglas.

The completion of the Canadian Pacific Railway and offers of land by the Department of Immigration attracted a flood of people. Almost overnight, Winnipeg became the busiest, rowdiest town in Canada. By 1885, the sound of construction echoed through its streets night and day to satisfy the ongoing demand for homes, hotels, bars, retail stores and warehouses.

Only in the model town of Broadway was the sale of lots for residential or industrial use almost non-existent. Southwest of Portage and Main, though the land was dry and high enough to avoid flooding, the throngs of newcomers found the HBC reserve property too expensive to buy. They simply didn't have the money to pay hundreds, even thousands of dollars

Left: International Association of Bridgeworkers / Provincial Archives of Manitoba / N-10981
International Association of Bridgeworkers / Provincial Archives of Manitoba / N-10979

28

to build their homes. They chose, instead, to live and work in the city's west end or, in the case of immigrants from Eastern Europe, in Winnipeg's north end.

The new immigrants brought with them incredible social change. Manitoba's admittance into Confederation in 1870 initiated a wave of young Anglo-Saxon Protestant immigrants from Eastern Canada, who quickly outnumbered the largely French and Metis Catholic population of Red River. The newcomers from Ontario brought strong cultural and religious biases that continued to exist in the city for decades, affecting where and how people lived, where they worked and how they were educated.

The last decade of the nineteenth century saw the first step toward the multiculturalism of Winnipeg, as tens of thousands of men, women and children came from around the world to find a new life in a city where change seemed the only constant.

The lethargy toward business on south Main Street finally ended in the late 1880s with the development of "the flats", the land at the junction of the Red and Assiniboine, by the Northern Pacific and Manitoba Railway (see page 69).

And though it would never be a town by that name, the Hudson's Bay Company's dream for Broadway finally came true as mansions and luxury apartments sprang up along the boulevard and cross streets leading to the Assiniboine River.

Provincial Archives of Manitoba / N-825

Magnificent homes, such as George Galt's mansion at Broadway and Donald, soon lined the boulevard and adjacent streets.

The Real Fort Osborne Barracks

Alfred E. Newman /Provincial Archives of Manitoba

For nearly fifty years mounted soldiers were a common sight on Broadway.

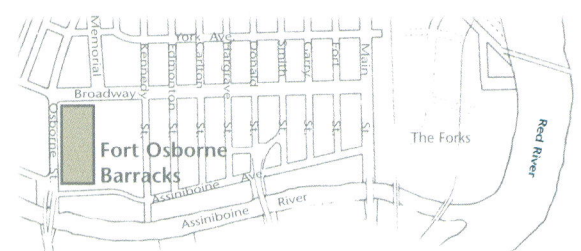

It's difficult to imagine today, but in 1872 what is now a very central location, the western half of the Legislative Grounds, seemed remote from the fledgling city's business section. It was, therefore, a perfect place to build Manitoba's new military headquarters. Construction of a new barracks was required after the military establishment at Upper Fort Garry was demolished when the Hudson's Bay Company transferred its vast North West fur trade empire to the Canadian Government in 1869. Built on twenty-five of the fifty acres of land set aside for public development under the terms of the transfer, the military complex was constructed within four months to house a contingent of 300 soldiers. Some had come west in 1870 with the Wolseley Expedition to

The Real Fort Osborne Barracks

Soldiers in the Winnipeg Light Infantry mass in front of the drill hall at Fort Osborne. The photograph was likely taken in 1885 prior to the regiment's departure for Saskatchewan and the Battle of Batoche. Lt. Col. William Osborne Smith (inset) remains an enigmatic figure, both praised and rebuffed.

maintain "peace, order and good government" and some were local militia who responded to Orange agitation in Ontario over the actions of Louis Riel's provisional government. Riel had resisted Manitoba's entry into Confederation without prior negotiations on the rights of the existing settlers, particularly those of the Metis.

Once the Manitoba Act had passed in 1870 and Manitoba became a province in Confederation, the move to the new site on Broadway got underway.

Soon twenty-four one-storey wooden buildings were spread out across raw unplowed prairie and bush. Walking today's lushly landscaped grounds, with its Manitoba Peace Plaque, and Holocaust and Next-of-Kin Memorials, it's difficult to envision the drafty huts of 130-odd years ago.

The Assiniboine River is still here, of course, bordering the site's south side, and Broadway, then unpaved but already in use, edged its north side. But little else remains. On the east of the new post was a lane behind Manitoba's second Legislative Building, then under

The Lord Strathcona Horse on parade beside the streetcar tracks on Broadway about 1900. Behind them, the Manitoba Legislative Building can be seen on the left and the drill hall on the right of the photograph.

construction, while to the west was Colony Creek.

Commanding the post was Lt. Col. William Osborne Smith. An Irishman who had come west with the Wolseley expeditionary force, he had remained in Winnipeg as adjutant-general of North-West Military District No.10, after General Garnet Wolseley and his regular troops returned to Ontario.

Recognized as an "energetic and active officer", Smith had served with rifles regiments in India and Montreal and in his ten-year command in Winnipeg he raised and commanded the 91st Winnipeg Light Infantry regiment that fought in the 1885 Rebellion.

In *Making of the West*, a book written in 1898, Rev. R.G. McBeth reports that "the men in the regiment enlisted from every nation under heaven. They were adventurers from every point on the compass who hailed the Rebellion as a great windfall. Many had served in General Gordon's Relief Expedition in Egypt. There were Indians, Irish, Scots, Icelandic, German, French and local students."

A popular leader among Wolseley's men and his mounted regiment after 1871, Lt. Col. Smith's middle name was selected as a suitable choice for the new barracks, for it linked the old fort and its new commander. In 1881, when Colony Creek was filled with the earth that had been excavated for the foundation of a new Hudson's Bay Company retail store at Main Street and York Avenue, the resulting roadway was named Osborne for its proximity to the barracks.

In the nine years before Colony Creek was filled in, a walking bridge stretched across to what is now West Broadway. At its western end, brothels sprang up and two enterprising proprietors, Shea and McDonagh, established a brewery.

In time the barracks were expanded to provide accommodation for officers and rank and file soldiers, and the base grew to include a hospital, recreation room, sergeant's mess, canteen, two washrooms, two cookhouses, a bakery, fifteen latrines and a guard house. A drill house and powder magazine for the artillery, a produce garden to feed the troops and a stable and cattle shed were added later.

But life was hard for the ordinary soldier, as it was for most residents of the Red River community. Crowded into one of ten hastily built wooden huts, next door to three huts the same size used by the department of immigration, as well as an armory, two clothing stores and the officers' quarters they endured frigid winters and sweltering summers.

Improvements were made in the mid-1880s. A large wooden drill hall set on cedar piles was built with two square front towers and an elliptical roof. In 1907, a two-storey building with stone dressings and a stone basement was added. It housed a coal bin and a furnace which heated a new guard room, offices and store unit. Next came quarters for eight married couples, each with a living room, verandah, bath and water closet.

The barracks remained on the Broadway site until 1913, when the Manitoba government contracted with Kelly and Sons to build a new Legislative Building and asked the federal Department of Public Works to vacate and move the complex. As no decision had been made for a new site by the time World War I began, some of the buildings were used until war's end.

Demolition of the buildings finally began in 1919, and the drill hall burned to the ground in a fiery blaze the same year. Earlier, a decision had been made to move to the Manitoba Agricultural College property in Tuxedo, where provincial architect Samuel Hooper designed a $250,000 barracks. The new building was initially used until war's end in 1918 as a hospital for wounded servicemen returning from World War I.

In the 1920s, a new brick and stone Fort Osborne Barracks was built at Corydon Avenue and Kenaston Street; seventy years later, this complex was remodelled and renovated to become Asper Jewish Community Campus.

Lt. Col. William Osborne Smith retired from the army in 1881, apparently without a pension, but remained in Winnipeg until 1884 to serve as manager of the Winnipeg Water Works. He planned to establish a dairy business in Carman but died in 1887 while visiting Wales.

While commander of Fort Osborne Barracks, Smith was elected the first president of the Manitoba Club in 1874. For reasons that remain a mystery, however, until recently his name was not listed on the roster of club members that hangs in the club hall. Michael Cox, retired manager of the Manitoba Club, found this oversight intriguing and attempted to discover why Smith had been expunged from club history. Alas, he was unsuccessful and the reasons for the soldier's long absence from the official roster remain a mystery. Although Smith's name now heads the club roster, an oil painting of A.G.B. Bannatyne also designates him as first club president.

Looking south from the roof of the old Law Courts building on Kennedy, Fort Osborne stretches into the distance in 1894.

Gathering Place *of the* Merchant Princes

Simple columns support the Manitoba Club's rather prosaic entrance, protecting by its very ordinariness the elegant interior from prying eyes.

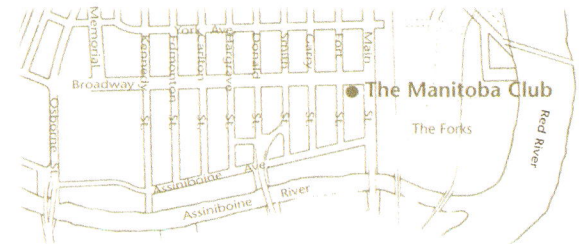

An aura of wealth and comfort still exists within the four-storey red tapestry brick Manitoba Club at Broadway and Fort Street. Oak panelled walls and staircases, deep leather-covered armchairs and thickly piled carpets – all the accoutrements speak of the Edwardian age in which they were first arranged in the clubrooms and lounges in 1905. But over the fourteen decades since the first private men's club in Western Canada was founded in 1874, its traditions and social attitudes have undergone radical change.

The menus have evolved from trenchermen style eight-course dinners to lean five-course meals. The prices have changed too. In 1879 the menu offered, for 60 cents, soup, fish, a choice of kidney sauté or minced veal and poached eggs and an entrée of roast loin of beef, roast

Gathering Place of the Merchant Princes

chicken, or boiled leg of lamb. Sweetbreads, spring chicken, plovers on toast, lamb chops or tenderloin steak could be added for 30 cents. The cheese selection included roquefort or stilton and a choice of grapes, melons, oranges or bananas. A glass of beer or whisky with water cost 10 cents; ginger ale was priced at 37 cents. Today a five-course meal with hors d'oeuvres, liquor and wine costs nearly $50.

Membership now stands at about 700 in all categories (active, non-resident and occasional). And members are no

Architect John D. Atchison, who also built Devon Court at Broadway and Edmonton, conceived a design that was, at least on its exterior, solid and businesslike, epitomizing the club's membership.

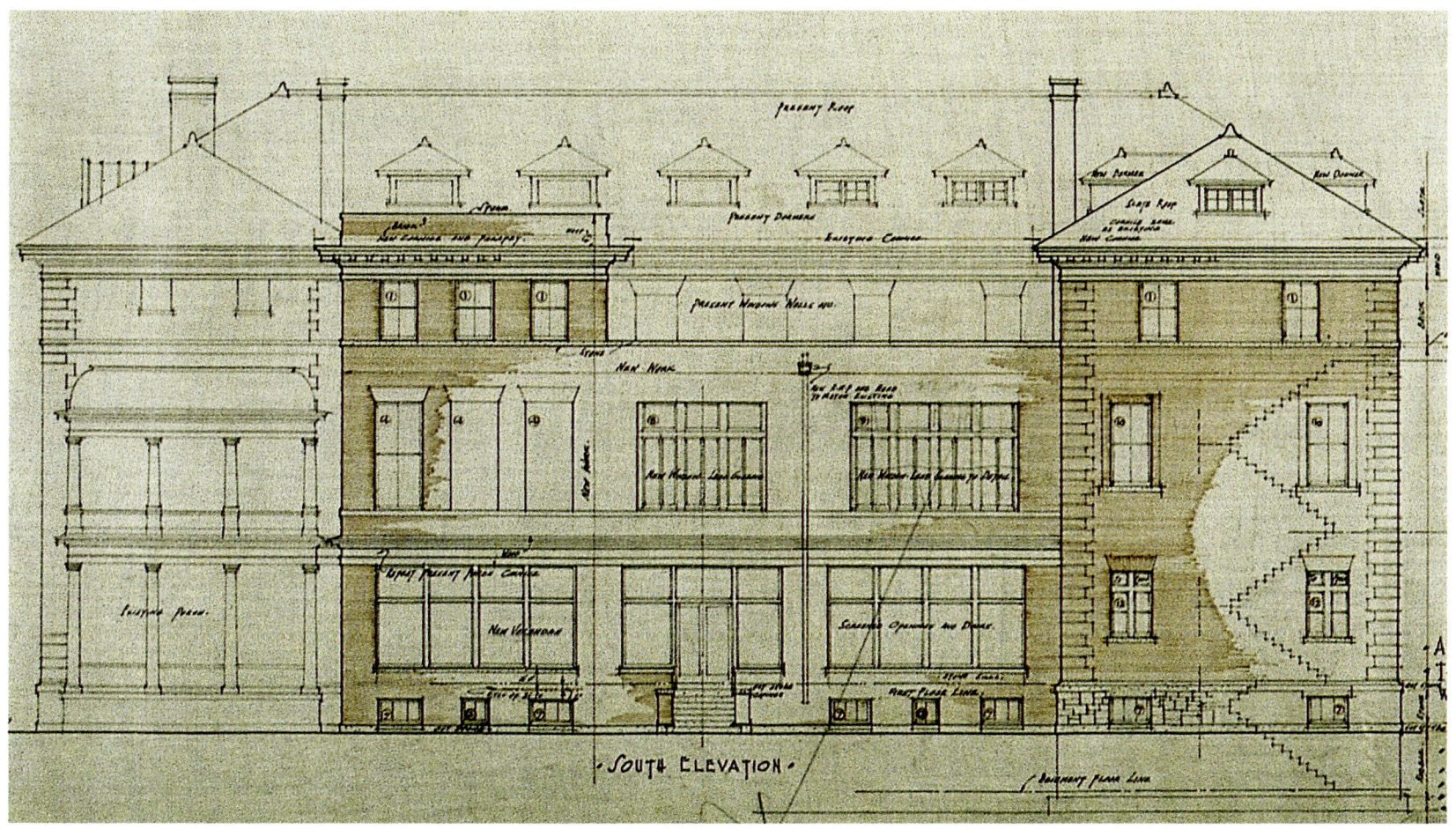

Street of Dreams: The Story of Broadway

A Not-So-Civil Skirmish

William (later Sir William) Van Horne was posted to Winnipeg in 1882 to serve as general manager of the CPR in charge of construction of the prairie section of the railway, from Winnipeg to Calgary. For the first few months of his residence in the city, he lived at the Pacific Hotel at the corner of Broadway and Main Street and, not surprisingly, soon became a member of the Manitoba Club, which was then located on Garry Street.

While dining at the club one evening in 1882, Van Horne was verbally assaulted by Major General Thomas Lafayette Rosser, the CPR's chief engineer whom he had fired that day for selling privileged information to speculators. Rosser later returned with a gun, threatening to shoot his former boss, but club members intercepted him and eased him out of the building before he could do any harm. Immediately remorseful, the general wrote such a charming letter of apology that everyone forgave him.

Both Van Horne and Rosser were Americans, but with very different backgrounds and temperaments. Van Horne was born in Chelsea, Illinois, in 1843 and left school at the age of fourteen to work as a telegrapher with the Illinois Central Railroad. An enterprising man of great versatility, he was superintendent of the railroad's Milwaukee line by the time he was twenty-seven. During the American Civil War, he fought on the Union side, and later immigrated to Canada.

When his mission with the CPR was completed, he pressed the company to develop telegraph and express services in the late 1880s, launched the Empress steamship line travelling between the Orient and Canada and helped to plan both the Banff Springs and Frontenac Hotels. He also negotiated the Crow's Nest Pass agreement. He was knighted by Queen Victoria in 1894.

Rosser was a southern firebrand who was a classmate of (General) George Custer at West Point. He fought for the Confederate forces in the Civil War before seeking greener pastures in Canada. He is said to have died a destitute postmaster in the American South.

Provincial Archives of Manitoba / N–8460

Above: Thomas Lafayette Rosser;
Left: William Cornelius Van Horne

longer restricted by gender, race or religion. Perhaps the most extreme change came in 1997 when women were at last welcomed into this male domain. Obviously, for decades many members had felt as did *Winnipeg Free Press* publisher E.H. Macklin. When it was proposed, in 1924, that mixed dinner dances be held at the club once a month, Macklin vehemently protested.

"Pray understand me. I defer to no man in my regard for and adoration of women – certain types of women – but I believe in women being confined to their proper places and a woman's place, I submit, is not within the precincts of a men's club," he said. "I speak strongly because I feel deeply. I love this building, every nook and cranny of it. It is to me a home, an asylum, a refuge. To it I come for relaxation. For bodily repose, for spiritual rest – by reason of the fact it is immune from the presence of women. It may seem an ungracious thing to say, but is true. I am firmly convinced that if once women are permitted to pass our threshold from that time the charm and indefinable atmosphere which surrounds and clings to a man's club will be lost for all time.

"I glory in the progress women have made. I rejoice in the liberty they enjoy ... I appeal to you to preserve one little spot on this planet where the swish of women's skirts and the music of their voices are not heard. It is not much of a boon to ask, but would prove a great boon to many of us – who for an hour or two every now and then want to live the simple life."

The resolution was initially defeated "overwhelmingly", though many men qualified this by saying they were not at all against women; indeed they agreed every man should own one.

But Macklin lost the battle later when the "headstrong gay Lotharios" won approval for an experimental dance and, subsequently, for other occasional dances where two orchestras played and the "salutary agility of the fox trot and the nimbleness of jazz" were the order of the day.

In 1929, Macklin again admitted he was licked when he bowed to a decision that a Ladies Section be added to the building with a special entry on Fort Street. Entry at the front door was denied to the ladies until 1979, when the ruling was removed for security reasons. Surprisingly perhaps, given the reaction of the likes of Macklin, Manitoba led the British Commonwealth in granting women suffrage in 1916.

Founded by a group of "gentlemen, scholars and judges of good whisky", who sought to share camaraderie, goodwill and friendship, the Manitoba Club has survived through depressions, wars and changing social attitudes.

The original goal was to find a place for companionship away from the rambunctious saloons and rowdy hotels along Main Street. To a man, the members longed for space to play cards or a game of billiards in a frontier town where felted slate tables were at a premium.

In the twenty-first century, this tradition continues. The club has six billiard tables where extremely competitive games are played by members every Saturday morning. There are also six or eight tables for bridge, but the poker tables are stored away in the attic. Cigars were banned in 1990 and smoking is allowed today only in specified areas, a dramatic switch indeed from 1898, when an order was sent to the Anglo-Egyptian Cigar and Tobacco Company for 6,000 cigars, 2,000 of them to be gold tipped and all to be marked with the club monogram.

Equally distant is the time remembered by Chief Justice E.K. Williams, who reminisced at the 1954 annual dinner about two club members with gargantuan appetites. They sat down "to imbibe a gallon and a half of burgundy and champagne, no uncommon feat five, four, even three generations ago."

into the undeveloped West. Those accustomed to amenities common in the cities of eastern North America and Europe found they were all but non-existent in Manitoba. Andrew McDermot, retail merchant "prince" of the Red River village, offered the lower floor of his Red River Hall, located at what is now Main Street and Lombard Avenue, as the first club quarters. Seven months later the timber-dry two-storey wooden building burned to the ground, despite efforts by the city's first manned steam fire engine to save it. Lost in the fire were the club's uninsured furnishings and a billiard table worth $1,000.

Undeterred by the disaster, the members soon rented a house on south Main Street, where they remained until 1881. That year, the popularity of the club in a city where men outnumbered women two to one prompted the membership to build a stately $18,000 brick clubhouse on the west side of Garry Street between Portage Avenue and Graham Avenue. The YMCA and saloons along Main Street were the only other facilities to offer such recreational diversions.

T he club was founded on July 12th, 1874, at the St. James Restaurant. At that founding meeting, members of the province's first Legislative Assembly gathered together with army officers who had come west with the Wolseley Expedition and single men from eastern Canada and the United States, all in search of adventure and an opportunity to make money in a frontier town. Lieutenant Colonel William Osborne Smith, Adjutant-General of the Northwest Territories, Military District No. 10, was elected first president.

Rich and poor, men from all professions and all walks of life had swarmed

At the time, the club roster included 150 members: prominent politicians from all levels of government as well as leaders in law, banking and transportation, land development, construction, retail sales and the military.

For the next seventy-five years they were the community leaders who controlled what happened in the city. Even today many of their descendants are the movers and shakers and backroom decision makers in Winnipeg.

Gathering Place of the Merchant Princes

Charter members included general store owner A.G.B. Bannatyne; one of Manitoba's early bank owners, Gerald McMicken; Henry T. Champion, founder of the first private banking house in the city; speaker of the first legislature and lieutenant governor of the North West Territories Joseph Royal; James McKay, a Metis and private contractor for mail delivery in the West, and Manitoba's high sheriff for fifty years, Colin Inkster.

Others among the membership soon included W.F. Alloway, a private banker and founder of the Winnipeg Foundation; Daniel H. McMillan (later Sir Daniel and lieutenant governor of Manitoba), and Hugh John Macdonald, son of Sir John A. Macdonald, a lawyer and judge who became premier of Manitoba in 1899.

In a sense the club served as a bellweather of Winnipeg's boom and bust years, the membership dropping as the economy slumped, the roster reviving as the city's population and business soared. The founding year, 1874, heralded the good times, but 1884 introduced a five-year depression in the community not long after the members had settled into their new quarters.

The new furnishings served notice that the club hoped to establish a tradition of elegance. And there were, of course, billiard and card tables. A chef was hired and the bar stocked with fine wines and liquors. But as the economy slowed, the club was faced with financial crisis. Fees went unpaid as tradesmen clamored for payment of their bills, and in 1887 there seemed a strong possibility that the Manitoba Club might fold. Even a project to install "water closets" was set aside.

Bank loans and the issuing of debentures kept the club afloat until the completion of the Canadian Pacific Railway brought an influx of newcomers from eastern Canada, the U.S. and

Interior views by Dennis Fast; Exterior by Peter St. John

Interior views of the club, from left, the main hall with the club crest at the far end; dining room settings; billiards awaiting players; the fireplace in the Buffalo Room and a sampling of the club's photographs and artwork. At right, the clubhouse as it approaches its 100th birthday.

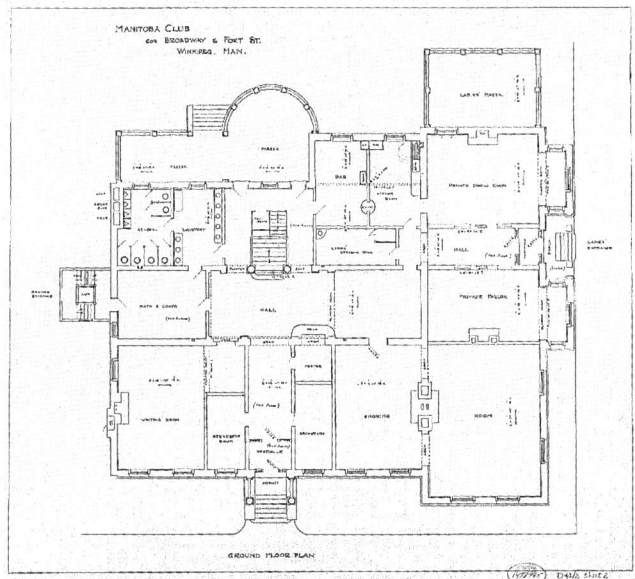

The architect's plans for the main floor of the Manitoba Club. Another wing, which included additional billiard, card and committee rooms, was added on the east or left hand side in 1909.

Europe. With them, prosperity returned to Winnipeg and the city's entrepreneurial businessmen renewed memberships, club bills were paid, and another generation of men found friendship and camaraderie at the Manitoba Club. In 1897, to celebrate the return of good times and the sixtieth anniversary of the reign of Queen Victoria, a special subscription was issued among members for the creation of a commissioned stained glass window – the Jubilee Memorial Window.

As the good times rolled into the new century, plans were made for another move, to an even more imposing red brick building on three lots purchased from the Hudson's Bay Company at the corner of Fort Street and Broadway. This new clubhouse, which still houses the membership today, was officially opened by Governor General Earl Grey in October 1905. Not surprisingly, membership soared.

The new building at 194 Broadway had spacious rooms for dining, billiards and cards, as well as for reading and business discussion. Trophy heads (at least one still hanging) adorned the walls of the Buffalo Room and other lounges. And architect W. A. Peters made provision for the removal and retrieval of the Jubilee Window from the old clubhouse, installing it prominently on the hall staircase.

The "old boys", the members who had nurtured the club through its exciting formative and difficult adolescent years, must have felt great satisfaction to see the crowds of younger men who now gathered at the new facility. Some even stayed there. Several rooms on the third floor were available until the 1980s to non-resident private club members from other cities. And one Manitoba Club member lived in one of the suites for almost fifty years, at the exceedingly reasonable rent of $60 a month, until he set fire to his room while smoking. Accommodation was found for him in a residence for senior citizens. Today, there is no overnight accommodation at the club. Upstairs, on the fourth floor, three rows of tiny bedrooms (now empty) housed the club's staff.

Changes to the facilities over the years have shown a remarkable focus on the club's original purpose and design. The east wing was added in 1909, with expanded billiard, committee and card rooms. Prior to World War I, a telephone switchboard was installed, but a proposal for a baseball diamond on nearby property was "emphatically rejected". In 1982, a spa facility was established in the basement, with exercise and steam rooms as well as change rooms with showers and lockers. And in 1995, though the entire ground floor of the west wing was gutted and renovated, the resulting decor is faithful to the traditional character of the club and would very likely meet the approval of its original members.

Little else has changed, other than eliminating the "ladies entry" and welcoming female members to the club. The club is no longer open Saturday or Sunday during the summer, or on Sundays during the winter, but the decor is much as it has always been, the food and service are still first class and the club prides itself on its wine cellar. In a club history published in 1995, it was touted as, "without doubt one of the finest [clubs] in Western Canada".

Perhaps inspired by its Jubilee Window, the Manitoba Club also has an excellent and growing collection of fine art. Building on a nucleus of paintings donated by William Alloway to the Winnipeg Foundation in 1930, with the proviso that they hang in the Manitoba Club as long as it remained a "first-class" institution, the club sets aside $10,000 a year for the acquisition of additional art.

There is also a certain attachment to what might be called memorabilia. Though letter carriers no longer drop by twice a day, as they once did, to pick up mail, the old metal mail box has been saved in its original spot by the front door and some members even drop notes in it. And the club's crest in wool broadloom, the centrepiece of a custom milled Irish carpet that graced the main lobby between 1959 and 1979, still hangs there today.

Despite the changes, the Manitoba Club retains an "old boys' club" aura, an ambience that ambitious young professionals, male and female, continue to find attractive. And for many, it still provides the refuge from the stress that E.H. Macklin so vehemently sought.

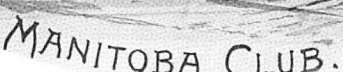

Viewed from Fort Street about 1908, the club looks unbalanced without its east wing and rather stark without the mature elms that surround it today.

Albertype Company / National Archives of Canada / PA-31534

41

Government House

Peter St. John

The mansard roof and ornate cupola of Government House are as distinctive today as they were more than a century ago.

Government House, traditional home to Manitoba's lieutenant governors, who serve as the Queen's representative and head of state, sits on 1.5 hectares of land adjoining the Legislative Building property at Kennedy Street, just north of the Assiniboine River. The house was first occupied in 1883 by Manitoba's fourth lieutenant governor, James Cox Aikins. Soon after, curious Manitobans had a chance to attend a New Year's Day reception to view the new house and sample a buffet of turkey, chicken, partridge, duck and venison. The tradition is echoed in today's New Year's Day levées.

A stately mansard-roofed, three-storey building designed by architect Thomas Scott, the house was built at 10 Kennedy Street in 1882-83 of quality white brick with a foundation and window sills of Stony Mountain

Government House

limestone. Described by architects of the era as "Victorian style, with Second Empire French influence, modified to suit the requirement of the climate", Scott's design complemented Manitoba's brick and stone Legislative Building, located at the time on the west side of Kennedy Street.

Thanks to the sturdy oak pilings and concrete footings set down to compensate for anticipated shifting in Winnipeg's unstable clay soil, it is one of the few mansions completed in the 1880s to remain standing more than a century later.

Using $23,995 in funding from the federal government, Government House was built to serve as a residence for the lieutenant governor and his family, as well as a vice-regal office and centre of provincial hospitality.

By 1885, $89,325 had been spent by the federal government on the house, outbuildings, grounds and furniture. That year Prime Minister John A. Macdonald transferred the house to provincial ownership with a stipulation that it "be used for no other purpose than the residence of the Lieutenant Governor".

The house was actually the fourth residence of its kind in Manitoba. HBC governor's houses were located at Lower and Upper Fort Garry between 1820 and 1870. And when Louis Riel established a provisional government in 1869, he took over the Upper Fort Garry house at

This 1877 painting of the Governor's House at Upper Fort Garry shows Lieutenant Governor and Mrs. Alexander Morris about to depart in the family's carriage.

After J. Penrose / National Library of Canada / C–18063

Street of Dreams: The Story of Broadway

Lieutenant Governors of Manitoba

Sir Adams George Archibald 1870–1872

Alexander Morris 1872–1877

Joseph Edouard Cauchon 1877–1882

James Cox Aikins 1882–1888

Sir John Christian Schultz 1888–1895

James Colebrooke Patterson 1895–1900

Sir Daniel Hunter McMillan 1900–1911

Sir Douglas Colin Cameron 1911–1916

Sir James Albert Aikins 1916–1926

Theodore Arthur Burrows 1926–1929

James Duncan McGregor 1929–1934

William Johnston Tupper 1934–1940

Roland Fairbairn McWilliams 1940–1953

John Stewart McDiarmid 1953–1960

Errick French Willis 1960–1965

Richard Spink Bowles 1965–1970

William John McKeag 1970–1976

Francis Laurence Jobin 1976–1981

Pearl McGonigal 1981–1986

George Johnson, M.D. 1986–1993

W. Yvon Dumont 1993–2000

Peter M. Liba 2000–

Dennis Fast

the junction of the Red and Assiniboine Rivers and renamed it Government House. Until then, the governor's houses at the two forts were occupied by successive Governors of Rupert's Land, who administered the Council of Assiniboia, a legislative body in charge of the affairs of settlers living in Hudson's Bay Company territory.

The third governor's house was a log home rented by the federal government for Sir Adams George Archibald, Manitoba's first lieutenant governor. Archibald was appointed by Prime Minister Macdonald in 1870 after the HBC had transferred its Rupert's Land territory to Canada.

Adams Archibald refused to live at Upper Fort Garry during his years of tenure. With heavy Victorian furniture, he found the house too small and instead spent his abbreviated term at Silver Heights, eight kilometres west of the fort. Located in what is now the suburb of St. James, Silver Heights was the home of Donald A. Smith, a provincial and federal politician who was also resident governor of the Hudson's Bay Company and chief commissioner for Canada. Smith, incidentally, is best known today as the man who drove the last spike to complete the Canadian Pacific Railway. He later became Baron Strathcona and Mount Royal.

Widely censured for shaking hands with Louis Riel, Archibald resigned in 1872. His successor, Alexander Morris, moved back with his family to Upper Fort Garry.

Manitoba's present Government House, the fifth oldest in Canada, has twenty-three rooms, including three reception salons, a state dining room, an assembly room and eleven bathrooms. Three narrow windows form a lantern light above the double oak front door to illuminate the stairwell and grand inner hall, where a curving oak staircase leads to the second floor.

Its U-shaped driveway is a memento of a time when horse and carriage brought dignitaries and guests to receptions and balls at the vice-regal residence. Its spacious grounds are lush in summer with colorful flowerbeds, and the house is sheltered in winter by oaks and pines. Flowers for gardens and plants for Government House are grown in an attached greenhouse.

Since 1883, all Canadian governors general, many prime ministers, heads of state, diplomats and numerous members of the royal family have visited or stayed at Government House. But the stringent security required to protect distinguished guests today means that

TO PAGE 46

Government House

The Office of Lieutenant Governor

The main job description for the position of lieutenant governor includes opening, proroguing and dissolving the Legislative Assembly, swearing in the premier and cabinet ministers and ensuring that a government is in office at all times.

But though the role is mainly symbolic and carries no absolute power, it demands a great deal in terms of time and personal attention. Definitely no job for the weak in body or spirit, the appointment demands intelligence, resourcefulness, flexibility and a readiness to deal with challenges. A diplomatic mindset and a knowledge of protocol are definite assets.

Official duties include delivering the Speech from the Throne, which customarily outlines proposed legislation, programs and initiatives of the government for each session. If a serving premier dies or resigns, the lieutenant governor must see that the post is filled immediately. He or she is also responsible for giving royal assent to and signing all bills passed by the legislature before they become law, as well as appointments of such government officials as deputy ministers, provincial judges, members of boards, agencies and commissions, crown attorneys and justices of the peace.

On occasion, a lieutenant governor can also advise a premier that a proposed new law or amendment is not viable. Such counsel was given to Premier Edward Schreyer in the early 1970s by the Honourable W. J. McKeag concerning changes to the Manitoba Schools Act.

Every lieutenant governor is paid a salary and, since 1976, a small pension at the end of his term. He is also provided with a house allowance to cover the cost of entertainment and travel in the province.

During his years of tenure, he can expect frequent visits from foreign dignitaries and will often play host to state dinners as well as luncheons, coffee parties and teas for people of all ages and all walks of life. Twelfth Lieutenant Governor W. J. Tupper attended 2,200 public functions in the first three years of his tenure in the 1940s and during the six years Jack McKeag was lieutenant governor, from 1970 to 1976, a total of 3,600 visitors signed the Government House guest book.

Then there are all the awards to be made, as well as funerals and church services, and cultural, sports and other events to attend. Added to every vice-regal agenda are regular tours to communities in the province to visit relief centres in times of emergency, or to call on hospitals, senior citizens homes or centres for the disabled.

Once appointed by the governor-in-council on the recommendation of the prime minister, for a period of not less than five years, the lieutenant governor can expect no change to his office without the unanimous approval of all provincial Legislative Assemblies and the Senate and House of Commons in Ottawa.

Even after retirement, every lieutenant governor and his or her spouse carries the title of "the Honorable" for life and is addressed as "Your Honor" in correspondence and conversation.

Dennis Fast

in-house stays rarely occur and hospitality is limited to state dinners in the formal dining room or receptions in the salons or the assembly room. Royals and foreign emissaries now stay in Winnipeg's downtown hotels. The Royal Suite on the second floor has become the vice-regal chambers.

On the main floor the Manitoba Room, which was originally the office of the lieutenant governor until quarters were built in the Legislative Building in 1920, is now a reception area. Here, visitors may sign the guest book and view the mahogany library table from which King George VI broadcast his address to the Empire in May 1939. In the same room, American broadcaster H.V. Kaltenborn launched an appeal to Canadians to buy war bonds in the early 1940s.

For 125 years Government House has welcomed members of the judiciary, the clergy, the cabinet, the consular corps and the armed services to a New Year's Day social gathering – or levée as it is called in the western provinces.

The tradition of public celebration to mark the New Year has deep roots. In 1877, Ojibwe Chief Kishekoka sent a letter to Lieutenant Governor Edouard Cauchon, in which he outlined his plan to visit Cauchon on January 1st, "as this is the day of the year which we and our forefathers have always kept since the white men came to our country – to shake hands and to smoke the Pipe of Peace in token of our friendship. We also pray you will give us counsel with regard to some grievances that we have and hope that you will use your influence for us with the Government of Canada."

Though the house retains the decor and attributes of a Victorian mansion, major changes have been made to it over time. Gone are the basement kitchen and servants' dining room. A dumb waiter (which once broke, sending hot food plummetting down the shaft) is no

longer in place. The kitchen was moved upstairs when Roland McWilliams was lieutenant governor in the 1940s, and a spacious serving area was installed during the tenure of Dr. George Johnson in the 1990s. A conservatory was added to the greenhouse designed by Walter Chesterton in 1886 and when motor cars replaced horses and carriages, the stables were torn down. A woodshed, icehouse and washhouse were demolished as heating, refrigeration and washing appliances became outdated.

A ballroom and verandah, added to the house by Lieutenant Governor Daniel McMillan at his own expense in 1901, was torn down in the late 1950s and replaced by the present assembly room. McMillan planned to entertain the Duke of York and Princess Mary

Dennis Fast

(later King George V and Queen Mary) in royal style during their stay at Government House. His plans were dashed by the death of Queen Victoria, which was followed by a year of mourning. The room then served only as a banquet hall where the female guests donned gowns in the semi-mourning colors of black, grey or purple.

Dawn McKeag established a library of literary works by Manitoba women authors in a new sunroom built off the state dining room when she was Government House chatelaine in the 1970s. A portrait gallery of photographs of all lieutenant governors since 1883 was introduced by Doris Johnson when she was chatelaine from 1986 to 1993.

While most lieutenant governors have donned British court uniform (also known as the Windsor uniform) at formal ceremonies and receptions, Jack McKeag, lieutenant governor from 1970 to 1976, is the only one pictured in regalia among the photographic portraits. The costume includes a cocked hat with a white plume, navy tunic, breeches and white stockings. Some vice-regal appointees prefer to wear a black morning coat and striped trousers on formal occasions. Lieutenant Governor Yvon Dumont, a Metis, added a woven sash about his waist (a *ceinture fléché*) when he donned the uniform.

From left: The mahogany library table in the Manitoba Room; the sweeping staircase to the second floor; a view of the dining rooms and, far right, the Victorian influence in the main floor salons.

Changes to staff duties and salaries have undergone the greatest change since the house was built. Gone are the days when a chauffeur, a cook and five maids were paid $1.75 each for a day's work, as they were in 1898, or 75 cents for an evening's work.

Today Government House operates on a ten-year budget plan in which costly repairs are carefully scheduled. The house is currently staffed by a house manager, the lieutenant governor's executive-secretary and a live-in housekeeper. Two women assist with cleaning the house twice a week and casual help is only hired to serve at social gatherings where 100 or more guests are expected.

A step into the three main floor salons is a return to the Victorian era, when Chippendale and Empire style furniture, brocade and velvet upholstery were *de rigeur*. Arranged on gleaming oak floors, the mahogany and burl walnut chairs, tables, cabinets, storage chests and sideboards present a picture of Winnipeg society home decorating preferences during the city's period of growth at the turn of the century.

Today it is almost impossible to find anyone to maintain or repair the 125-year-old eight-bell mahogany Westminster grandfather clock that stands in the front entry. The same exceptional craftsmanship common to the 1880s is also seen in a nearby Victorian wardrobe of plain and burl walnut. A 1906 oil painting of bison on the prairie by Frederick A. Verner, a Canadian artist and friend of Alexander Morris, Manitoba's second lieutenant governor, recalls life on the prairies more than a century ago. The painting was discovered in the 1960s by Lieutenant Governor Errick Willis' son in the Government House flag tower.

In the state dining room, a crystal chandelier hangs over a magnificent mahogany dining table where forty-two guests can dine. Its length can be further extended with a table from the small dining room. Manufactured by the Chippendale family in Britain about 1770, the dining suite was purchased by Sir Daniel McMillan during his term of office. It was later sold and purchased by S.H. Kilgour of Winnipeg, who then loaned it back to Government House during the tenure of Lieutenant Governor Richard Bowles. In 1970, the Manitoba government bought the table and twelve chairs.

In the adjoining small dining room, where the vice-regal family enjoys its daily meals and entertains informally, a round walnut Victorian table is surrounded by ebonized walnut chairs.

Nearby, an early Victorian china cabinet of plain and birdseye maple was originally used as a bookcase upstairs.

In the state dining room ornate objects such as an 1860 French ormolu (brass made to look like gold) clock and candelabra set, an 1850 antique coffee urn engraved with the crest of 1934–40 Lieutenant Governor W. J. Tupper and an 1850 centerpiece combining a flower arranger with the candelabra and Waterford crystal bowls can be seen.

A silver tray on the sideboard in the small dining room is believed to be the oldest known piece of Canadian-made silver in Manitoba.

An 1885 brass curat stand, which can serve as a cake stand or a plant holder, an antique Chinese screen and an 1865 hand blown glass centerpiece from England are also found here.

A porcelain sculpture of Chief Wankan Tonkan by Manitoba artist Helen Granger Young in Salon One was presented to mark the House's 100th birthday in 1982. Joe Fafard's ceramic sculpture of "Emmett", his elderly neighbor in Pense, Saskatchewan is found in Salon Three. After seeing "Emmett" while visiting Winnipeg, comedian Bill Cosby commissioned Fafard to create three sculptures of himself.

As a visitor to Government House, Cosby is in good company. Since 1870, at least twenty-one British royals and every presiding governor general have visited the vice-regal residence. Others who have stayed at or visited the house since 1883 include French actress Sarah Bernhardt (who had tea with Lady Aikins in the 1880s); World War II British Prime Minister Winston Churchill (while on a speaking tour in Canada in 1901); American composer and bandmaster John Phillip Sousa; Sir Robert Baden-Powell, founder of the Boy Scout movement, and Lady Baden-Powell, as well as singer and variety star Gracie Fields.

Since 1970, visitors have included South African writer Sir Laurens van der Post, Princess Christina of Sweden, British High Commissioner to Canada Viscount Derek Heathcoat Amory, Canadian author Margaret Laurence, 1975 Nobel Peace Prize winner Dr. Andrei Sakharov and his wife Dr. Yelena Bonner, Roslynn Carter, wife of former US president Jimmy Carter, Nobel Prize winner Mother Theresa and Vigdis Finnbogadottir, president of Iceland. Canadian astronaut Roberta Bondar, former American First Lady Ladybird Johnson and American evangelist Billy Graham have also been Government House visitors, along with American entertainers Liberace, Harry Belafonte and Sammy Davis, Jr.

Government House, as it must have appeared when Manitoba's fourth lieutenant governor, James Cox Aikins, first occupied it in 1883.

49

The Stately Homes of Broadway

As the twentieth century rang in, Broadway was the most fashionable residential district in Winnipeg. Wealthy businessmen lived in handsome family homes on property the Hudson's Bay Company had initially reserved to become a model town for the well-to-do (see page 22). Reserve lots were large and expensive and could not be subdivided, eliminating them as housing alternatives for most newcomers to the city.

After an intitial period during which the neighborhood was largely overlooked, it gained popularity with the city's richest powerbrokers in the mid-1880s. Soon it became the place where Winnipeg's elite socialized in mansions on Broadway itself and along the grid of streets between Main and Kennedy adjacent to the Assiniboine River.

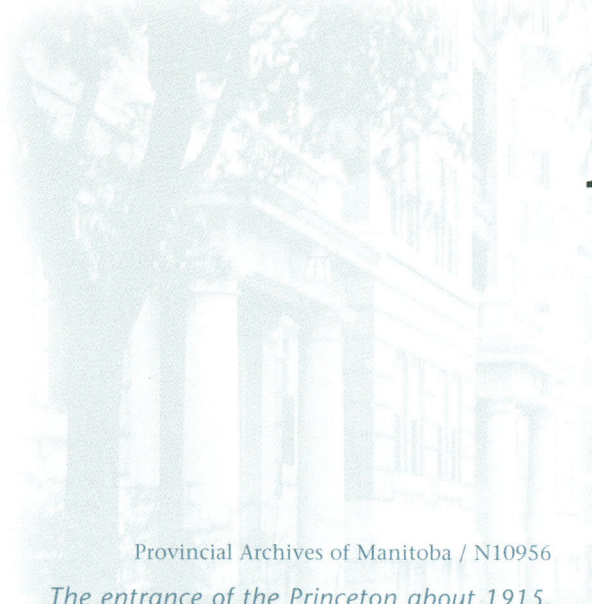

Provincial Archives of Manitoba / N10956

The entrance of the Princeton about 1915. When it opened in 1909, it was described as "grand" and "self-confident".

The Stately Homes of Broadway

Hardware mogul James H. Ashdown lived there in a three-storey home with a tower. So did manufacturing and mining tycoon Thomas Black, Senator David Walker, Lieutenant Governor James A. M. Aikins and Sir Hugh John Macdonald (Manitoba premier in 1899–1900), as well as barrister F.W. Thompson and realtor Thomas Bell.

By 1902, the trend to luxury apartment living so popular in major American cities caught fire in Winnipeg as land developers built four- and-five-storey blocks designed with five- and six-room suites along the wide boulevard.

In 1909, the Princeton apartment building was Winnipeg's tallest skyscraper, its five storeys towering over the young elms that lined the boulevard. Today, the Princeton is the last residential remnant of Broadway's five once-grand apartment blocks.

By 1912, four more impressive apartment buildings were in place between Garry and Kennedy Streets. None was less than four storeys high and all were constructed with the highest standards in plumbing, lighting, ventilation and fire safety. They all had elevators and most suites had fireplaces.

An address on Broadway signalled social approbation, for the district was safe and well landscaped, close to a neighborhood of middle-class west end family homes and far distant from the impoverished North End ghettos.

In the neighborhood's heyday, residents included warehousing and grain trade officials, wealthy widows, academics and railway executives. TO PAGE 54

Three years after designing the Manitoba Club, architect John D. Atchison created Devon Court, with its popular O'Devon Court Cafe for residents and their guests on the fifth floor.

After Provincial Archives of Manitoba / N-676

Dalnavert

If a house can be said to resemble its owners, Dalnavert is an uncanny reflection of the couple for whom it was built. Sir Hugh John Macdonald, the only surviving son of Sir John A. Macdonald and briefly premier of Manitoba, was serious, bookish and introverted, a man who, one senses, came reluctantly to political life. His wife Gertie, by contrast, was outgoing, sociable and artistic, a woman who loved fashion and design and was a noted hostess.

Dalnavert's English-born architect, Charles H. Wheeler, managed to combine elements of these two personalities in his design at 61 Carlton Street. It combines a solid, sensible brick exterior with unexpected, almost frivolous accents of limestone and Virginia long leaf pine. The limestone forms window caps of several different shapes, while the pine wraps around the main floor in a sweeping verandah ornamented with circular motifs that are repeated inside the house. Officially, this combination of masculine structure and feminine accoutrements is classified as Queen Anne Revival, but in it Wheeler combined features of High Victorian and Art Nouveau styles. In an article entitled "A Perfect Home" that he wrote for *The Winnipeg Tribune* in December 1895, just months after

Today, Dalnavert is expanding its horizons to interpret life in 1895 Winnipeg more broadly. A new interpretive centre is planned, which will explore such ideas as Victorian sensibilities and food production as well as music, sport and social life.

the house was completed, he described it as a "modern colonial style".

Inside, the juxtaposition continues, with cedar intricately carved to reflect the light, large rectangular windows ornamented on top with stained glass, and solid newel posts, one of which is topped with a bronze figure.

Dalnavert was one of the first private homes in Winnipeg to include all the latest "mod cons" – electric lighting, indoor plumbing, central hot water heating and closets in many of the rooms. The original wiring was so new and experimental that it had to be completely replaced just four years after the house was built, to comply with newly developed safety standards. The new knob and tube wiring was the type installed in houses for decades to come.

Hugh John Macdonald, a lawyer who had been elected leader of the Manitoba Conservatives in 1899, became premier of the province that same year. His tenure was brief, however, for he was soon induced to resign to run federally in the 1900 election. He had been convinced, perhaps by his former law partner J. Stewart Tupper, that he might be a successor to Tupper's father, Sir Charles Tupper, as prime minis-

A view of the interior, showing the intricately carved woodwork.

ter. Alas, Macdonald chose to run in Brandon against Clifford Sifton, one of Canada's ablest politicians, and was defeated.

Though no stranger to politics, having been elected federally in 1891 and served in Tupper's short-lived government of 1896, Macdonald may have been secretly relieved by the outcome. He once said that were he to suddenly come into a million dollars, he would happily flee politics.

In any event, he retired from public life following his defeat, and the next year found time to be involved in a renovation and redecoration of Dalnavert that the newspapers termed "lavish". Seven years later, the large house was again redecorated and the family continued to live on Carlton Street until Hugh John's death in 1929. Lady Macdonald moved to the Roslyn Court apartments and for the next decade the house was either vacant or used as a boarding house. Sold as a boarding house in 1940, by 1957 Dalnavert contained no fewer than seventeen suites.

Finally, sold again and threatened with demolition to make way for a high-rise apartment complex, Dalnavert was saved by the Manitoba Historical Society in 1970 and restored to its original 1895 beauty.

Since then, regular repairs and occasional renovations have achieved an even more authentic result. Thanks to a tireless corps of volunteers, it continues to offer a glimpse of the lives of a privileged Winnipeg family more than a century ago.

Dalnavert was designated a Provincial Historic Site in 1988 and a National Historic Site in 1991.

Street of Dreams: The Story of Broadway

> On August 26, 1930, Winnipeg was the site of the largest conference ever to be held in Canada, as more than 900 doctors gathered for the 98th annual conference of the British Medical Association. On Sunday, the delegates marched down Broadway to attend church.

They shared a milieu that echoed New York's Park Avenue, with its European-style boulevard and nearby private men's club, the Manitoba Club. Both were firsts in Western Canada. There was even a tiny park that surrounded the Governor's Gate, the last remnant of Upper Fort Garry. Proximity to the business hub at Portage and Main also meant apartment dwellers could walk to work or hop on the electric street car at their doorsteps.

Designed by eminent architects, each apartment building made a distinctive statement. Local newspapers described them as "grand", "theatrical", "monumental", even "self-confident". They displayed pillars, symmetrical facades and parapets. Some boasted cornices or pediments. Others had glassed-in porches and most had ornate lighting fixtures of burnished brass as part and parcel of every suite.

Today, all but two of the five exclusive apartment complexes built between 1902 and 1912 are gone. Broadway Court was torn down in the 1940s; Fort Garry Court, the first to be built, burned in 1976 and Devon Court was demolished after St. Stephens Church burned in 1981, badly damaging the apartment building next door. It was torn down the following year.

Still remaining is the Princeton's neighbor, the forty-three suite Strathmore (renamed the Atholl) at 326 Broadway, but it no longer serves as an apartment block. Instead, it has been converted to an office building housing consultants and government agencies in its upper three storeys, and two haute cuisine restaurants, Amici and Bambolini, on the first floor and lower level.

The Princeton (called The Kenmore until 1928) still stands at 314 Broadway, adjacent to the southeast corner of Hargrave at Broadway. It was built in Beaux Arts style in 1909 at a cost of $200,000. A landmark for the city, it was designed by William Wallace Blair, an Irish architect who also drew plans for many Exchange District banks and warehouses that still stand today, as well as the Roslyn Apartments on Osborne Street, the Warwick on Qu'Appelle Avenue and a number of character homes in Crescentwood.

As solid in structure as the day it was built, with not a crack in the foundation or brick walls, the Princeton today has lost its luster. Its brick and concrete exterior needs deep cleaning, its two courtyards are grungy, its windows sooty from car and bus exhaust. Inside, the yellowing varnish of its oak-panelled foyer walls, the expanding metal inner door of the elevator (once opened only by an attendant) and a foot-wide strip of ceramic tile embossed with the name "Princeton" hint of Broadway's glory days. Only one five-room suite, complete with a working wood fireplace, remains.

The rest of its original fifty-five apartments have been sectioned into eighty-one two- and three-room suites. Most are inhabited by students, who along with a number of long-time residents, live amid the vestiges of an era when the citizens of Winnipeg believed that their city would soon be bigger than Chicago.

A grand renovation would be neccessary to restore the Princeton. But such a renovation might be just

University of Manitoba Faculty of Medicine Archives

The Strathcona on Main Street and Broadway, better known as Fort Garry Court after its enormously popular restaurant, is reported to have used cut stone from Upper Fort Garry for its foundations.

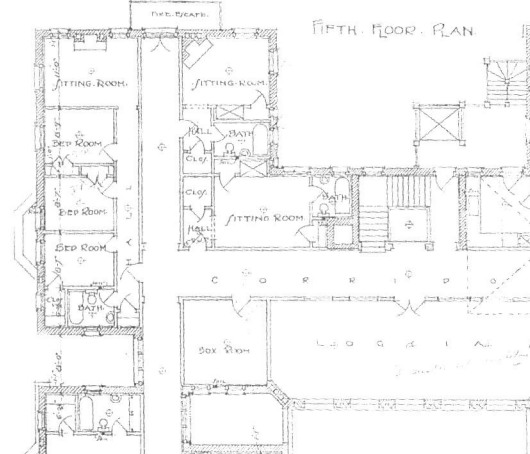

The fifth floor plan of Devon Court shows bachelor suites without kitchens. The young professionals who lived here took their meals in the dining room located on this floor.

the catalyst to draw people with a taste for urban living downtown.

Broadway Court at 251 Broadway, on the northwest corner of Garry, was built in 1906. Designed by architects Alexander and William Melville for owner Geoffrey Malton at a cost of $75,000, the four-storey buff-colored brick building had a dentilled cornice. Verandahs in suites across the front of the building were duplicated on the inner three sides of the courtyard.

Devon Court, at 376 Broadway, was a model for gracious living and luxurious comfort with fifty-seven suites. Built in 1908 at a cost of about $200,000 at the south east corner of Edmonton, it was designed by John D. Atchison. Built of stone and concrete, in the shape of a U, Devon Court's five- and six-room suites were fashionable and roomy with little extras in decor.

With the exception of the fifth-floor apartments, which were bachelor suites with no kitchens, each apartment included a parlor, dining room, two bedrooms and small kitchen. At Devon Court a doorman was on hand twenty-four hours a day and the O'Devon Court Cafe, for residents and their guests, was located on the fifth floor.

Fort Garry Court, at Broadway and Main Street, was once the site of an uncompleted hotel built in 1872 by a consortium headed by Donald Smith, the one time HBC Governor, who was later knighted as Lord Strathcona.

Its stone foundation collapsed in 1875, with a similar catastrophe bringing down its successor, the Pacific Hotel, in 1882, impoverishing consortium members. The ruins of the building sat at Main Street at Broadway until 1902 when Smith built an opulent thirty-four suite apartment block, the Strathcona, on the site.

An impressive brick creation designed in four sections with a square courtyard, it had a "commodious bar and billiard room". Its Fort Garry Court Cafe and Restaurant Service soon attracted the city's "high-class clientele".

This was the place where the wealthy went to dine and dance and be seen. Its kitchen was overseen by a chef known for his culinary skills in Paris, London, Sydney and Melbourne.

The suites were roomy and comfortable for the resident professionals, but it was the restaurant that caught the public imagination and by 1912 the building was known simply as Fort Garry Court.

Broadway's decline began soon after. As World War I ended, the district had begun to lose its standing as an upper class neighborhood. Broadway's millionaires (who numbered thirteen in 1913) were moving to Wellington Crescent, Armstrong Point or Crescentwood, where they built palatial new homes along the Assiniboine River. Over time Fort Garry Court's roomy suites were divided up, eventually numbering 200. Many of the tenants now were working class employees of the Canadian Northern Railway and Union Station. By the time it burned to the ground on February 2nd, 1976, taking the lives of five tenants, little remained of Lord Strathcona's original vision.

The palatial houses along Broadway soon followed suit. By the mid-1920s, a majority of the district's old mansions had become boarding houses crowded with tiny suites.

The red brick Schultz house at 271 Broadway, built in 1883 at the northeast corner of Donald for Sir John Schultz, (a pioneer businessman who became lieutenant governor) was home

The Stately Homes of Broadway

to boarders by 1919. The Union Center stands there now. The gabled house at 288 Broadway, on the southwest corner of Smith, built by general store owner Jerry Robinson in 1885, became a rooming house until 1955 when it was demolished to make room for the Investors Syndicate building.

Lindenlee, a three-storey gabled house named for the poplar trees in the yard (at 307 Broadway and Donald), was built for Grand Trunk Pacific Railway Commissioner Charles J. Brydges in 1879. Remodelled later into a charming apartment block of small suites, it burned down in 1945. A Safeway store was subsequently built on the site where a coffee bar and the Tweedsmuir Apartments now stand.

The red brick Ashdown mansion with its three-storey tower, built in 1897 on the northwest corner of Hargrave went through a series of metamorphoses after James Ashdown and his family moved into more palatial quarters on Wellington Crescent in 1913.

In its second incarnation it became the Conservative Association's Adanac Club, with a four-storey addition at the back. In the early years of World War I it served as the officers' mess for the 90th Winnipeg Rifles. Purchased by the Music and Arts Company for $10,000 in 1917, it housed the studios of the leading voice, piano and instrumental teachers of the time. In 1933 it was bought by the warden of St. John's College (then located on Main Street) to become St. John's College on Broadway.

It was torn down in 1962 to make way for the Monarch Life Building, now home to the Workers Compensation Board; St. John's College built anew on the University of Manitoba campus in Fort Garry in 1958.

At Carlton Street and Broadway, Albert Austin, the man who introduced both horse-drawn street cars and electric trolley cars to Winnipeg, built a white brick family home in 1892. In 1901 it became Havergal College for girls and in 1964 it was demolished soon after Riverbend Girl's School and Rupert's Land School combined to become Balmoral Hall, in the former home of Lieutenant Governor J. A. M. Aikins.

Pioneer surgeon Dr. Henry Chown lived nearby at 263 Broadway. An energetic, forceful man, he was described by a student of his, Dr. Gordon Fahrni, as one of the last surgeons in Canada to regularly operate without gloves. It clearly did nothing to hamper his effectiveness. The Kingston-born doctor not only served as professor of surgery at Winnipeg General Hospital for twenty-one years, but was Dean of Medicine, and president of the Canadian Medical Association in 1900–1901. A world traveller and dynamic speaker, he was also the father of Dr. Bruce Chown, who isolated the Rh factor, perhaps the most outstanding medical discovery ever made in Manitoba.

Dr. and Mrs. Henry Chown and their dog Rab were photographed on the porch of their home at 263 Broadway in 1903.

Above: Provincial Archives of Manitoba
Below: University of Manitoba Faculty of Medicine Archives

The Birth of a University

More than a decade after the University of Manitoba was created in 1877 by bringing together three denominational colleges – St. Boniface College, St. John's College and Manitoba College – to provide the entire teaching function for higher education in the province, it had no physical home. In fact, when it was established by legislative charter in 1891, it was purely a degree granting institution without powers to teach and subject to the control of the churches which had established the colleges, now numbering four with the additon of Wesley College in 1888. As a home of higher learning, this public university had no teachers, no classrooms, no labs and no student body. When the charter was amended in 1892, the university was given permission to teach, but no provisions were made for resources or

Lorne Thompson, courtesy of St. John's College

Before moving to Broadway, St. John's College was located in this ornate building at Main Street and Church Avenue.

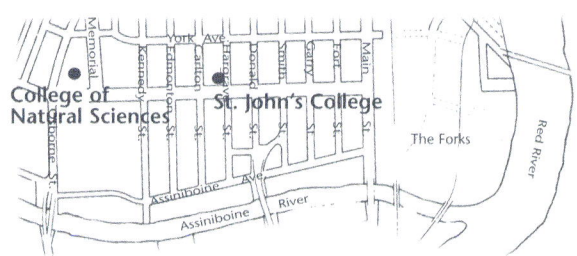

The Birth of a University

construction, apart from a cooperative deal with the four colleges to prevent wasteful duplication. Finally in 1901, the University of Manitoba lost its homeless status. A three-and-half-storey sandstone brick and Manitoba limestone building, designed by architect George Brown, was erected on Old Driving Park, (now Memorial Park) across from the original Fort Osborne Barracks at Broadway and Osborne Street.

Despite this physical presence in the heart of Winnipeg, there was anything but consensus on the ultimate site for the university. In fact, until the 1930s nobody, not the provincial government, the university administrators nor the university council could agree on where the campus should be permanently located. Would it be on Broadway, in Tuxedo or in Fort Garry? There were times when meetings must have sounded rather like an Abbott and Costello discourse on "Who's on first?".

In 1898, the Canadian government had transferred 6.6 acres (2.2 hectares) of property at Broadway and Osborne to the province for educational purposes. In 1901, $40,000 was spent to erect the buff brick building, with basement and facing details in limestone, on what was considered to be the most convenient location for the students, the public and the affiliated colleges to develop as an integrated institution. The Duke and Duchess of York (later King George V and Queen Mary) opened the College of Natural Sciences during their tour of Canada.

TO PAGE 62

After 1945, St. John's moved to Broadway and Hargrave, where classes were taught in what had been the Ashdown mansion. An addition, not shown, was attached to the rear of the house.

After Lorne Thompson, courtesy of St. John's College

The Founding Colleges

If the University of Manitoba is a relatively youthful institution, its three founding colleges – St. Boniface, St. John's and Manitoba Colleges – are considerably older. All three trace their roots back to the mid-nineteenth century. St. Boniface College officially originated in 1854, three decades after the arrival of Catholic missionaries in the Red River Valley in the 1820s. The first incarnation of the college was located near St. Boniface Cathedral when the charter to establish a Manitoba university was signed in 1877. That building was destroyed by fire in 1922 and the college moved to La Petite Seminaire, on nearby avenue de la

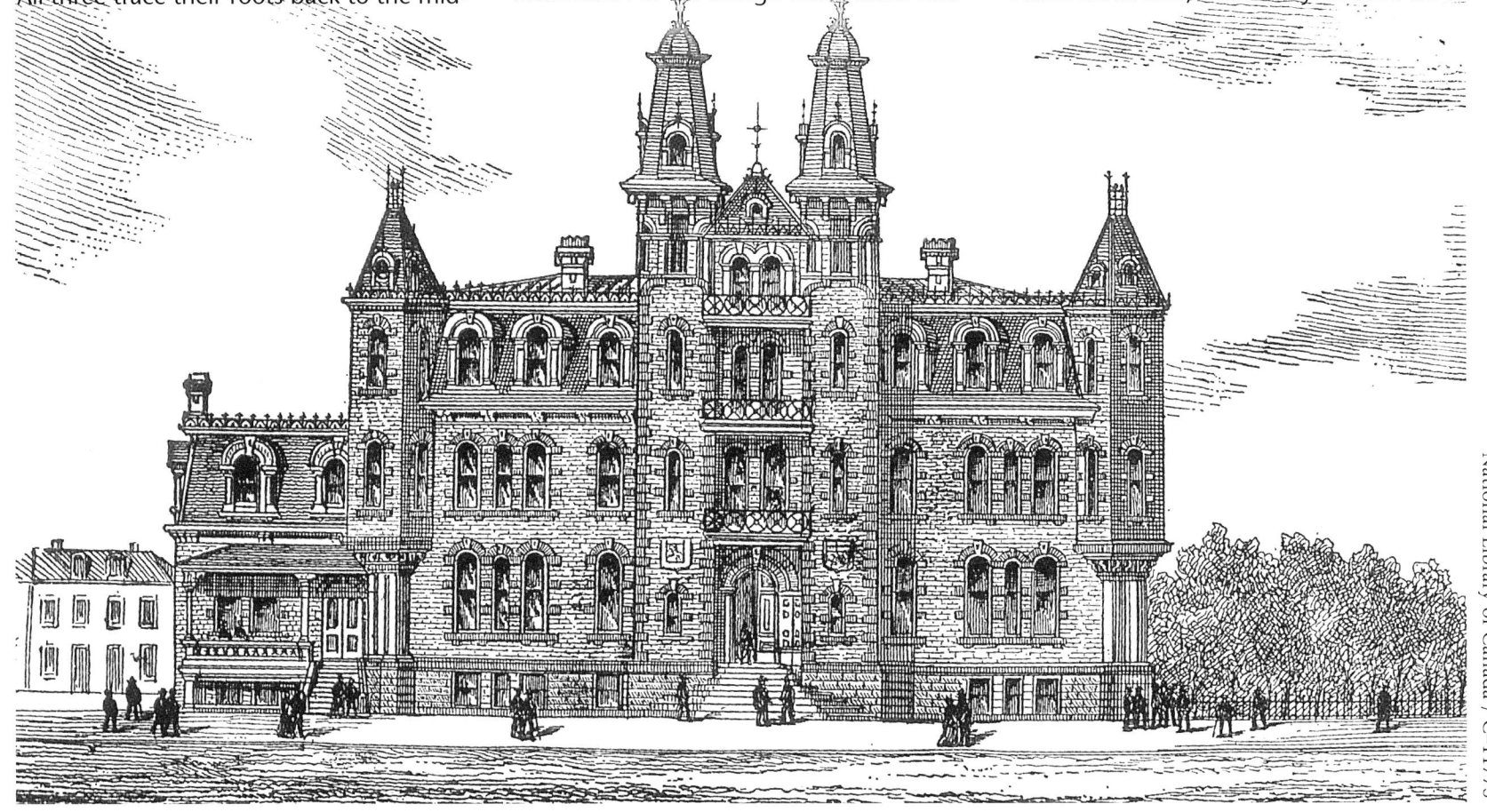

Though founded by sensible Scots Presbyterians, Manitoba College was housed for nearly fifty years in an elaborate Italianate building on Ellice Avenue, shown here in a drawing from 1882.

cathedrale, where it remains today.

The Anglican mission established in the Red River settlement in St Andrews Parish by John West in 1820 led to the founding of St. John's College in 1866. Initially housed in Red River frame buildings near St. John's Cathedral on the Red River east of Main Street, St. John's College Boys School moved to a handsome Revival-style brick and stone building at Main Street and Church Avenue in 1884. A further move to the Music and Arts Building on Broadway in 1945 (the original Ashdown mansion) preceded its relocation in 1958 to the University of Manitoba campus.

Manitoba College, founded in 1871, represented the Presbyterian faith of the Selkirk Settlers. Originally housed in a simple one-storey gabled structure adjacent to Old Kildonan Church, the college moved to a many turreted Italianate building on Ellice Avenue at Vaughan in 1881. After the union of the Presbyterians with the Methodists and Congregationalists in 1925, which created the United Church of Canada, the building was sold to the Oblate Fathers in 1931 and became St. Paul's High School for Boys, the first English Catholic secondary school for boys in the city. In 1931, St. Paul's became affiliated as a college with the U of M and joined St. John's and St. Andrew's Colleges on the Fort Garry campus in 1958.

There were other affiliations beyond the founding three. In 1888, Wesley College, a Methodist institution founded in 1873, became affiliated with the university, twelve years before building a Romanesque sandstone building on Portage Avenue. Wesley College subsequently became United College and has since become the independent University of Winnipeg.

The Manitoba College of Medicine was affiliated with the university in 1883 when its students were instructed in anatomy and medicine at Kate Street and McDermot Avenue. In later years, they moved to Bannatyne Avenue and Emily Street. And in 1899, the Manitoba College of Pharmacy became affiliated with the other colleges.

Today, all affiliated colleges except St. Boniface College, which maintains a francophone campus in St. Boniface, and the Faculty of Medicine downtown, are located on the Fort Garry site.

The first incarnation of St. John's College reflected the institution's fur trade roots in its simple Red River frame structure. Classes were taught here between 1866 and 1884.

Even this arrangement had its detractors, however. St. John's College, then located on Main Street, was dissatisfied with the site choice until an adjustment was made to provide free student streetcar fares.

The new building seemed to signal that Broadway was to be the future site of a University of Manitoba complex, but that conclusion bedevilled authorities for the next sixty years. The initial step in future site chaos was the purchase in 1902 by the government of Premier Rodmond P. Roblin of 117 acres (39 hectares) along the banks of the Assiniboine River in Tuxedo at a cost of $15,000. This was to become the site of an Agricultural College, "far and distant", according to its critics, from the city. The main building, a sandstone and Manitoba limestone structure in neo-Palladian style, was built in 1906. Today, it is part of Asper Jewish Community Campus, after serving as a military barracks and juvenile court for fifty years.

Despite these developments, the search continued for a larger site for the university. Plans were made by the government to expand the original land purchase in Tuxedo, where an administration building and 250 students were already in place. As an alternate to the Broadway location, they accepted an option of another 150 acres (50 hectares) near Assiniboine Park. The developer's focus was on the development of grand family homes. The university would be the educational feature of Tuxedo Park: the Suburb Beautiful.

However, when it was later suggested that all the colleges unite at the Agricultural College site, the Aggie administrators were opposed to the idea. They "believed that students of agriculture were diverted from devotion to their studies by association with other students at the university." They also felt "the college men were not sympathetic with the traditions and problems of agriculture."

Instead of being a move toward the development of an efficient system of higher education, the issue initiated a saga of divided effort, confused purpose and unbalanced financial commitments. With so many postsecondary education buildings interspersed in colleges on Broadway, in St. Boniface, on Main Street, Portage Avenue, Bannatyne Avenue and Ellice Avenue, as well as in Tuxedo, it was evident that serious decisions had to be made about exactly where the University of Manitoba campus should be permanently located.

Within five years the Tuxedo site had a problem. The college needed more field space at a reasonable cost. Once more the provincial government stepped in. In 1911, it bought 570 acres (188 hectares) of land eleven kilometers south of the city along the Red River in what was then St. Vital – today's Fort Garry campus site.

Two years later, the university council agreed to accept the government's offer of 113 acres (37 hectares) of the government land in Fort Garry and began construction of a number of buildings on the site: a neo-classical red brick and limestone administration structure and dormitory (now Taché Hall), as well as buildings for chemistry, physics, botany and dairy science.

With the onset of war in 1914, all plans for additional construction on the Fort Garry site were put on hold, giving Premier Tobias Crawford Norris a chance to request a return to the Tuxedo site as a permanent campus location. His government even approved a grant of $330,000 dollars for further building construction in Tuxedo.

In 1922, a new government under Premier John Bracken introduced a royal commission to settle the question. The commission advised, for both educational and financial reasons, that the Agriculture College and the university should be united in Fort Garry.

The Birth of a University

In 1924, the Agricultural College reaffiliated with the University of Manitoba as the Faculty of Agriculture and Home Economics and moved into the Administrative Building in Fort Garry for all its classes.

With the decision finally made, a university president, J.A. MacLean, was elected for the first time, an arts course was initiated, the pharmacy college became part of the university and the teaching of engineering was widened.

Nineteen twenty-four was also the year the university was sued by the F.W. Heubach Tuxedo Park consortium for not meeting its option agreement to build a campus on the site. The battle for a move back to Tuxedo was renewed by some university council members, while lawyers debated and students complained about their makeshift quarters, which had been built in 1909 on Broadway.

Construction of the ramshackle buildings had resulted from the inability of the government to come to a decision on a campus location. As a result, a helter-skelter arrangement of classrooms sprang up between the provincial jail and the Law Courts. Students mingled with gangs of prisoners who passed back and forth en route to the Law Courts, and their quarters were often shrouded

Lorne Thompson, from the Winnipeg Free Press, 2/2/46

When it came to proposals for a unified university campus, even the students got into the act. This plan is based on a model created by fourth-year architecture students in 1946. It involved closing the streets from St. Mary Avenue to Broadway between Donald and The Mall (now Memorial Boulevard) and creating an integrated urban campus rather like Northwestern University in Chicago.

in smoke erupting from the central heating station chimney.

The decrepit buildings had been assembled to cope with the increasing number of students enrolling in the sciences and the establishment of faculties in need of classrooms in the Broadway area. For example, the School of Architecture, founded in 1913, was housed in rooms in the old Law Courts building on Broadway near Kennedy. The Manitoba Law School, founded in 1914, held classes in the YMCA on Smith Street. Law students wrote exams in the Manitoba Hall on Portage Avenue; the School of Art and art gallery were in the Industrial Bureau's Exposition Building at Main Street and Water. Arts, science and engineering lectures were given in the old Law Courts and at the Institute for the Deaf at Sherbrook and Portage.

An educational authority from the Carnegie Institute, called in to report on the choice of a university site, commented: "As a place for eliciting the finer perceptions of young men and women through the educative influence of a wholesome and impressive environment this (situation) leaves much to be desired."

Student protests about having to work in "cow-sheds" reached a comical pitch when a cow was led up to the second floor of the old Law Courts building on Broadway and tied to the library door.

In 1930, the university settled with the Tuxedo developers and with the consolidation of both the Agricultural College and the university, two Gothic style arts (Tier) and science (Buller) buildings were erected.

A phased withdrawal from the Broadway site to Fort Garry was led by the graduate divisions and schools.

In the early years of the twentieth century, students such as these lacrosse players played on athletic fields in front of the College of Natural Sciences in what is now Memorial Park.

The Birth of a University

It began, in 1932, with the School of Architecture's move to the attic of the Tier building. However, the Depression and the outbreak of war in 1939 delayed the move of other major divisions to Fort Garry for another twenty years. It was not until 1960, therefore, that the old Broadway building was replaced at Fort Garry with three new buildings: the Armes, Allen and Parker Buildings.

During the late fifties, St. Paul's and St. John's Colleges were built. They were followed to the Fort Garry campus by the Schools of Art and Music, the Faculty of Education (formerly the Manitoba Teachers' College), and St. Andrew's and University Colleges. The neoclassical Faculty of Law (Robson Hall) was built in 1970.

Had anyone considered a 1908 re-development proposal for the Broadway area by layman town planner Leo Warde, the university site problem might have been entirely avoided.

The twenty-one-year-old Warde suggested that the Legislative Building be centered in line with Vaughan Street, which would be broadened to form a Mall. He envisioned the Legislative Building fronting on Broadway at one end and at the other end, on Ellice Avenue, a new City Hall on property then occupied by Manitoba College.

Warde's proposition was rejected in favor of one by architect John D. Atchison, who designed Devon Court (see page 56).

Atchison's plan called for a forty-five meter wide thoroughfare beginning at the 1882 Legislative Grounds on Broadway and Kennedy and ending at Portage Avenue. As well, Atchison's center point was farther west, emerging from a point on the western side of the Legislative Grounds. Nor did it include the relocation of City Hall.

Warde, who died in 1944 after serving as reeve of St. Vital, is best known as the originator of the Vimy Highway project in Winnipeg and is credited with the original idea for the city's Perimeter Highway. While the government and the university council dithered about the best site for post-secondary education in Winnipeg, life did go on for the students on Broadway. There were lacrosse, basketball, hockey, football and fencing teams. Beginning with fall fraternity and sorority parties, there were social events – dances and tea dances, dramas and choral performances.

There were also illustrious professors who expanded the minds of generations of students. Arthur Reginald Buller, professor and head of the department of botany, and Rupert Clendon Lodge, professor of philosophy, were two such men. Professor Buller's specialty was fungi, which led to the establishment of the Rust Research Laboratory here, when cereal rust destroyed grain crops in Canada during World War I. A scientific Sherlock Holmes, he used pen and ink illustrations and photographs, as well as infectious enthusiasm, to get his message across to a wide audience.

Born and educated in England and Europe, he joined the university in 1904 and soon found that he loved the Winnipeg weather and found it stimulated his research. He enjoyed good music, great literature, a game of billiards and crossing the Atlantic each summer, which he did sixty-five times before his death in 1944 at the age of seventy.

Professor Lodge was born in Manchester, England, in 1885. He developed a theory of comparativism in which he recognized the possibility of several points of view. Personally, he was an idealist, rather than a pragmatist and a lively, stimulating and popular teacher. His lectures were spiced with humor and to the end of his life he was always generous to those who had fallen on hard times and was an anonymous benefactor for many causes.

Gateway to the West

Responding to crowded highways and overburdened airports, Canadians are returning to the more leisured pace of rail travel. Today's trains, with updated amenities and a renewed focus on fine dining and first-class service, recall a bygone era when railways ruled the west. And Winnipeg's elegant and spacious terminal, with its intricate terrazzo floors and copper-domed rotunda, is one of the best places in the country to capture a period that many of us, sentimentally perhaps, believe was simpler and more straightforward.

Despite the elegant surroundings, the reality was often quite different. For decades, beginning in 1911, Union Station was jammed with jostling throngs of arriving and departing passengers. Winnipeg was the gateway to the West and a sense of excitement was always in the air. Day

Peter St. John

Situated just north of the main entrance, this charming portico is an indication of the attention to detail that marked the design of Union Station.

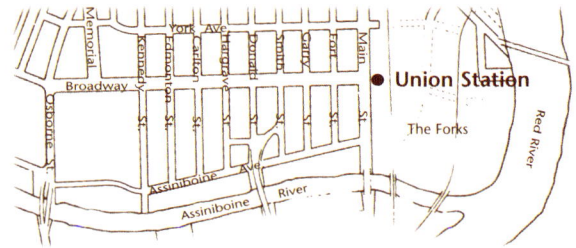

Gateway to the West

after day thousands of immigrants stepped off the trains to find a new life for themselves and a better education for their children. They came to work on farms and in factories and offices in a province that had become known as the Heart of the Continent or, lured by the promise of free homesteads, stopped en route to destinations farther west. For decades, the rumble of iron wheels on steel tracks and the lonely whistle of the engines could be heard day and night.

TO PAGE 70

That Union Station was a bustling, "happening" place from the day it opened is evident in this rendering, created about 1912.

Valentine & Sons / National Archives of Canada / C-148327

A Plethora of Railways

As a joint venture between the Canadian Northern Railway (CNR), the National Transcontinental Railway, the Grand Trunk Pacific Railway (GTPR) and the Dominion of Canada, the construction of Union Station symbolized the breaking of the national rail monopoly originally held by the Canadian Pacific Railway. It also heralded a new era of co-operation in the rail industry.

The CPR monopoly, granted by the federal government in 1880, had prohibited construction of any other rail line running south or southwest of the CPR mainline to any line within fifteen miles of the 49th parallel, assuring the company of financial success. But the newly-arrived farmers favored rail competition to

This overview of the station, photographed by the Department of the Interior in 1928, shows Broadway with its maturing elms, the railyards occupying the "flats", and the Red River and St. Boniface beyond.

improve service and lower freight rates. Winnipeg businessmen also regarded more lines as essential to the development of the West, and ultimately their own prosperity.

By 1888, the anti-monopolists had obtained the revocation of the monopoly and within fifteen years there were twelve branch lines entering Winnipeg. All railroad branch lines were chartered by an act in the Manitoba Legislature.

The Northern Pacific and Manitoba was the first railway to provide the kind of service and freight rates rural communities wanted. In 1888, NP and M acquired the flood-prone "flats", the land from the forks of the Red and Assiniboine Rivers west to Main Street and north to Water Street. To turn the low-lying area into a productive rail yard, the company added more than a metre of fill all along the Red River embankment. This not only raised the level of the land, it covered all traces of the long-term use of the area by many different cultures over the previous millennia – leaving a buried treasure for archaeologists to find a century later.

A rail yard at The Forks was a dream of both private developers and the Hudson's Bay Company, for it greatly enhanced the value of the adjacent land, which the HBC still hoped to sell and develop into a residential neighborhood.

Union Station under construction in 1909.

During the next few years, the NP and M blossomed, operating trains over 399 kilometres of branch lines from Winnipeg to the new towns springing up across the province, carrying thousands of immigrant homesteaders to farmland near Portage la Prairie or Hartney or as far south as the international border.

Four years later all the branch lines in the province amalgamated as the Manitoba Railway Company, which was in turn purchased by the federally owned Canadian Northern Railway, with its headquarters in Winnipeg. After buying twenty-four acres of land from the Hudson's Bay Company in 1903 to expand its rail yards and build a station, an agreement was made with the Grand Trunk Pacific Railway and the National Transcontinental Railway (both of which wanted a Winnipeg terminal) to share one facility. That facility, insisted the HBC, must be built no farther north than Broadway, though initially the railways wanted to be located closer to the main business district at Portage and Main.

The result, in 1911, was not only one of the largest railway centers in North America, but a stately Main Street bookend to the classic Legislative Building planned for Broadway and Osborne Street, and an eastern anchor for the treed boulevard of upper class homes and luxury apartments that bordered Broadway by the early 1900s.

The completion of Union Station also spelled changes for transportation of other kinds as the early water transportation system that had served the Red River settlement and the fledgling City of Winnipeg was soon replaced by railways, streetcars and automobiles.

An interior view of the main rotunda, with its inlaid terrazzo floor.

Through three wars (World Wars I and II and Korea), the rotunda reverberated with the sound of military bands bidding farewell to troops leaving for overseas or welcoming war-weary survivors home from combat. Despite the send-off, for many Union Station was a terminal of tears, where young men – and some young women – went off to war, an appalling number never to return.

All told, Manitoba's contributions to Canada's war efforts were enormous. In World War II, for example, more than 80,000 of the province's citizens – a disproportionate share of the population – had served in the army, air force or navy, some with great heroism and distinction, and all too many paid with their lives.

Between the wars, the stirring music of bagpipes echoed through the station from time to time as pipers welcomed visiting members of royalty or greeted Canadian prime ministers to Manitoba.

In the 1920s and '30s there were New Year's Eve parties, held at no charge in the rotunda, where local musicians played the popular tunes of the era for as many as 1,500 celebrants. One First Night gathering at the station listened to a chamber orchestra playing classical music.

Today, Union Station is a quieter place. Twelve trains a week travel the rails through Winnipeg – three from the east, three from the west and six heading north and south – three to Churchill and three returning. In an average year, slightly more than 40,000 passengers travel through Union Station, an average of about 110 a day. And in the echoing rotunda, it's hard to imagine the throngs of the past. On the July long weekend of 1920, for example, 8,000 people bound for Grand Beach boarded the trains here.

Constructed at the peak of the railway boom in Canada and amid the feverish growth of the city, Union Station opened to the public in 1911. Federal census figures show that the population of the city grew from 31,649 in 1896 to 163,000 in 1916, but the city's assessment figures record an even greater increase during the same years, according to urban historian Alan Artibise. In *Winnipeg: A Social History*, he quotes the city's figures for the same years as 37,983 (1896) and 201,981 (1916).

Built between 1908 and 1911 for the Canadian Northern Railway (CNR), Grand Trunk Pacific Railway (GTPR) and the National Transcontinental Railway (NTR), Union Station was designed by Warren and Wetmore, architects of New York's Grand Central Station. Its plan and classical details were based on the Beaux Arts style, architecture that typified the City Beautiful movement so popular in North America at the time.

An imposing structure built entirely of stone, the station runs 100 metres

Gateway to the West

Largely unchanged after 90 years, the centre block of Union Station is still imposing and solidly beautiful.

along Main Street with a width of forty-two metres. Its main entrance is at street level in the center of the building. In the Beaux Arts tradition, it has a three-part facade composed of a centre block and two rectangular wings. Since 1990, it has had Heritage Railway Station designation from the Historic Sites and Monuments Board of Canada.

The station is four storeys high with a basement and an elaborate rotunda lit by great arched windows on all four sides and a copper dome directly opposite the center of Broadway. The central Main Street entry is enclosed within an enormous arch flanked by a double column-and-pier combination on either side, projecting three metres beyond the exterior walls. Today, a sign on a parapet bears the name VIA; the parapet, which was built in the 1960s to hide the machine room above the elevator shafts, partially blocks the view of the dome.

The latest in early twentieth-century design, the station's innovative traffic patterns quickly moved passengers from ticket booth to baggage area, along an under-track subway and up to the train tracks. Passengers waiting for trains exited through the north side of the lobby to an adjoining 836-square-metre waiting room. A similar, but more direct plan is used today with the ticket counter adjoining space for coach, silver and blue class travellers, who go directly by escalator to the tracks, eliminating the need to climb the stairs down and then up to the platform.

But immigrant passengers had an entirely different view of the station in 1911, for this was an era when discrimination based on race, religion and language was prevalent. To serve the needs of immigrant passengers and yet maintain class distinctions, much of the basement area was devoted to huge waiting rooms, according to a front page report in the June 27th, 1908 edition of the *Manitoba Free Press*. One end had a

This impression of Union Station in February 1943 comes from the war diaries of Private Lamb.

lunch counter, a laundry and separate men's and women's washrooms, the other had a men's smoking room and a separate room for women. On arrival the immigrants were conducted to and from the waiting rooms and trains by stairways, which led directly from the basement to the passenger subway or to a separate "immigrants' entrance" off Main Street.

In a 1912 issue of *Railway and Marine World*, an article assessed the segregation of travellers this way: "It will therefore be seen that immigrants will be well provided for and will be handled to and from both trains and station without coming in contact with other passengers."

Today's basement facilities are quite different. The lower level houses a physical training center for VIA Rail employees, as well as tenant storage rooms. The upper floors of the station are occupied by Statistics Canada on the second floor, and Red River College on the third and fourth floors. On the main floor, the station's original lunch room, which covered 120 square meters, as well as a restaurant nearly twice that size on the north side of the waiting room, no longer exist. In their place are the federal government offices of Public Works, Government Services and Environment Canada as well as Manitoba Conservation.

Today, the ticket office is near the passenger waiting room, but originally it was located on the south side of the lobby. Balconies, set between ribs that arch upward to the dome, still overlook the gray terrazzo floor and the metre-high brown-and-tan veined marble wainscotting.

Lighting for the rotunda was once provided by ornate bronze sconces. Today's contemporary cylindrical tube lighting, as well as the plastic chairs and cafe tables may be more practical, but heritage officials consider them to be intrusive elements.

Yet despite these modernizations, Union Station at ninety is still classically beautiful. A stroll through the soaring rotunda and out onto Broadway can still elicit the same sense of wonder expressed by French artist Paul Maze, the man who taught Winston Churchill, among others, to paint. Arriving at Union Station the year it opened, Maze wandered through the rotunda and out the main entrance to gaze down Western Canada's first boulevard, lined with elms. To his artist's eye the view, apparently, was entrancing.

Years later in London, he recalled his vision of Winnipeg to a young university graduate about to take a position in Winnipeg. "I recall the station," Maze said. "An absolutely magnificent building. And beyond it, the panorama down the boulevard is one of the most beautiful sights in Canada. You must visit it as soon as you are settled. And give my regards to Broadway."

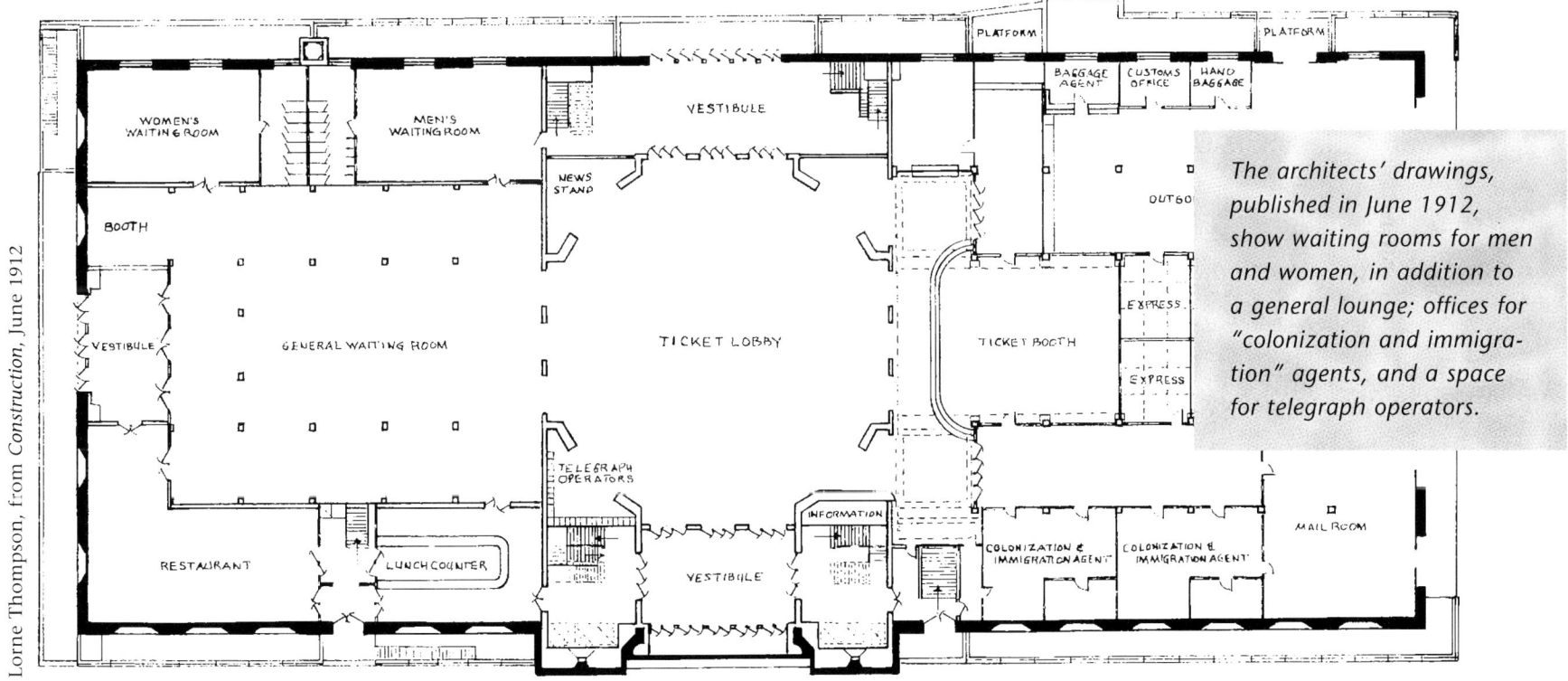

The architects' drawings, published in June 1912, show waiting rooms for men and women, in addition to a general lounge; offices for "colonization and immigration" agents, and a space for telegraph operators.

Blueprint for a Fantasy

There's a story that Walt Disney chose the design for his Fantasyland castle and his Magic Kingdom logo from a memory he carried of his first sight of the Hotel Fort Garry during a trip he took through Winnipeg as a young man.

It's certainly possible. In 1919, Disney returned home to rural Missouri following wartime service as a teenaged ambulance driver for the Red Cross in Europe. His most direct route was west across Canada to Winnipeg and south to Missouri. And anyone stopping at Union Station couldn't help but notice the hotel's copper-clad turrets, dormer windows and steep roof lines. Towering fourteen storeys above Union Station, they truly give the hotel a "fantasyland" appearance.

Peter St. John

The "Loire Valley chateau" design, evident here, was soon co-opted to become "Canadian-style architecture".

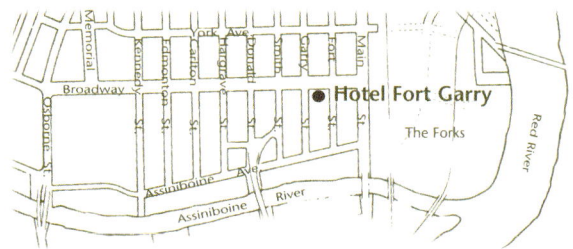

Blueprint for a Fantasy

There are other stories about the hotel that are not quite as plausible. One, concerning a tunnel that purportedly ran underground from the hotel to the station, to allow staff to transport banquet quality food to the waiting trains, is simply inaccurate. There is a tunnel, but it contains pipes laid in a slightly heightened crawl space under Main Street, which once conveyed heat from the station to the hotel. Today, an electrical power station near Higgins Avenue heats the station; the hotel is heated by both natural gas and electricity.

And then there are the hotel's ghosts, apparently benign creatures that

Anchoring the east end of Broadway, the Fort Garry, the Manitoba Club and Union Station gave the boulevard an aspect of grandeur by 1920.

Second-floor Spirits

Ontario Liberal MP Brenda Chamberlain had a ghostly experience at the Hotel Fort Garry in the autumn of 2000, when she was awakened by the sense of someone climbing onto her bed. Knowing that her husband was at home in Elora, Ontario, and finding herself alone in the room after turning on the light, she found it difficult to sleep. She was still awake at 2:30 a.m. when again she had an impression that someone was getting into bed. And again, after searching the room, even under the bed, she found no one in the room.

Chamberlain later learned that the "presence" she felt in the room was one of the hotel's most famous spooks – the bereaved widow. It seems that in the 1920s, a newlywed couple stayed in Room 202, which was Chamberlain's room that night. The young bride complained of a headache and her obliging husband went out to find some medication. Alas, he was killed on his foray and when his wife found out, she committed suicide.

Since then, it's said, her ghostly spectre occasionally sits on second-floor beds, still apparently in search of her husband.

Hotel staff members say other guests have also been startled several times in the last eight or nine decades, after experiencing a friendly, but rather disconcerting ghost, in some of the bedrooms. And still others have reported hearing screams from the kitchen, where someone, long ago, was supposedly decapitated. More recently, the banquet manager and other staff members have seen what seems to be a Celtic apparition standing in a corner of the Provencher Room. Dressed in a kilt and looking quite substantial, the figure has the rather disconcerting habit of disappearing when anyone approaches.

Fortunately, none of this has affected hotel business. In fact, every year a number of people reserve rooms at the hotel in the hopes of having their own close encounter with a ghost.

The spooky second floor.

have intruded upon some of the most sensible guests and, more recently, the senior staff at the hotel.

As Winnipeg's first skyscraper, the Hotel Fort Garry was built by the Grand Trunk Pacific Railway between 1911 and 1913. It was both the first commercial building to be erected on Broadway, and the last railway hotel to be constructed in Manitoba.

Set on a site that was as old as any settlement in the West, the hotel was built on vacant property that once lay just outside the walls of Upper Fort Garry. It was originally slated to be called the Selkirk, after Thomas Douglas, Earl of Selkirk, founder of the Selkirk Settlement that predated Winnipeg, but it was renamed due to its proximity to the old fort, which had been demolished in 1881. Parks Canada heritage specialists believe the property was probably the midden or refuse dump for Hudson's Bay Company fur traders at the forks of the Assiniboine and Red Rivers. And long before that, it's likely that early Manitobans had gathered here, at the confluence of the rivers, for millennia. So beneath the hotel's cavernous basements, all manner of secrets may be buried.

Located one block west of Union Station, which served both the GTP and

Canadian Northern railways until 1923, it opened in December 1913 to glowing accolades from the press. It was, according to one newspaper, "a stately building comparable to the beauty of the Acropolis". Lieutenant Governor Douglas Colin Cameron added that it ended forever the city's "pioneer" identity.

Described as "an adaptation of Francis I Loire Valley chateau" design, it was also reminiscent of the clean-cut architecture of the newly built Park Plaza Hotel in New York.

The Fort Garry was the second in GTP President Charles M. Hays' grand plan to build impressive hotels in major cities along the company's rail routes. His first venture into the luxury hotel milieu was the Chateau Laurier in Ottawa, built a year earlier.

Hays was emulating the success of the Canadian Pacific Railway in attracting tourists with its smart marketing, which evolved from the philosophy of company president William Van Horne. "If we can't export the scenery," Van Horne had said, referring to the magnificent vistas along the CPR route through the Rocky Mountains, "we'll import the tourists." And he began building a series of grand hotels in major railway centres across the continent.

As conceived by architects George Ross and D.H. MacFarlane of Montreal, the design of the Chateau Laurier used the popular "chateau design" (soon to be known as Canadian-style architecture) to create an elegant hotel worthy of the nation's capital. Even before it was finished, the Hotel Fort Garry was under construction and plans were drawn for two other hotels, the Macdonald Hotel in Edmonton, which opened in 1915, and Minaki Lodge, just north of Lake of the Woods in Ontario, completed in 1914. Minaki Lodge mimicked the CPR's success with rustic accommodation in such scenic spots as Jasper.

Unfortunately, Hays was a victim of the sinking of the *Titanic* in 1912. His death, the onset of World War I two years later and the depression that followed the end of the war combined to delay future hotel construction by the GTP indefinitely.

Appearing remarkably blasé, given the height and angle of their work space, a small army of roofers took a break from sheathing the hotel roof with copper to pose for this 1913 photograph.

Street of Dreams: The Story of Broadway

It was only after 1923, when the federal government nationalized the GTP and Canadian Northern Railways as an amalgamated Canadian National Railway, that the company's network of railway hotels began to expand again, under the CNR's first president, Sir Henry Thornton. Soon, other hotels sprang up to accommodate travellers in castle-like surroundings during stopovers right across Canada.

Constructed of steel frame sheathed in Indiana buff limestone over a gray granite base, the Fort Garry was situated "away from the noise and dirt of the Portage Avenue and Main Street business section". The same light colored stone was used in building the Chateau Laurier.

Its construction consumed 2.8 million bricks, 500 cords of stone, 56,000 square metres of plaster, and 3,700 cubic metres of concrete. The basement is a remarkable three storeys deep and each storey has granite walls six metres high. Today, the first level contains a modern stainless steel and ceramic tile kitchen, as well as a separate kosher kitchen; the next level down houses an immense laundry, while the bottom level is used for storage.

During the 1960s and 1970s, as inexpensive motel accommodation increased, the Fort Garry went into decline. The City of Winnipeg seized it in a dispute over back taxes in 1983 and finally, in January 1987, its doors were locked. That year, Quebec hotelier Raymond Malenfant rescued the hotel from demolition, but later defaulted on the seven million dollar mortgage held by the Laberge hardware empire. Again, the future of the grand hotel seemed in doubt.

Enter Richard Bel and Ida Albo, a pair of economists who were former owners of the Prairie Oyster, the Sandpiper and Du Bon Gout at The Forks. In 1994, they entered a fifty-fifty partnership with the Laberge hardware family of Montreal to restore the Fort Garry to its original splendor.

Bel and Albo had fallen in love with the hotel during the years they catered special events for their restaurants using the Fort Garry's kitchen facilities. They agreed to refurbish the lobby and 246 guest rooms, where necessary, with a $1.5 million investment from Laberge.

That proved to be only the beginning. To date several million dollars more have gone into restoring the hotel to its early splendor. Today, from the main lobby, with its Caen stone floor

Blueprint for a Fantasy

inset with Napoleon gray marble, to its magnificent seventh-floor ballrooms, the Fort Garry makes a clear statement that a heritage luxury hostelry has been reincarnated in Winnipeg.

The Crystal and the Concert Ballrooms (the latter with a stage) and their adjoining hallways and loggia are resplendent with replicas of the paint and wallpaper from the hotel's first years. Plaster moldings have been recast; modern techniques have been used to reapply gold leaf and the original light fixtures have been rewired.

Long windows, inset into exterior walls in both ballrooms are sparkling; the original stained glass inserts of the provincial coats of arms in the Concert room and of famous composers in the Crystal Ballroom are in mint condition - just as they were on the day they were placed in the wooden window frames. The huge wooden ceiling beams have been lovingly restored by fifty skilled workmen hired for the two-year project.

Similar renovations to the hallways and loggia have been carried out under the trained eyes of Toronto restoration expert David Hannivan and Interior Illusions co-owner Magda Zelikson of Winnipeg, but only after the pair pored over architectural plans and old photographs to ensure each detail was correct.

In the dining room and fifteen meeting rooms, the faddish innovations of the 1960s have disappeared, replaced by a faithful recreation of the original elegant Edwardian atmosphere. The Drummer Boy Lounge has been reborn as the Palm Room, exactly as it was

From the majestic main lobby, far left, seen here from the mezzanine, to the beautifully refurbished hallways and the magnificent Concert and Crystal Ballrooms, the Hotel Fort Garry has been faithfully restored to its original grandeur. The result allows Manitobans, along with visitors from across North America and abroad, an accessible taste of early twentieth century elegance. They have responded by making the hotel a favored place for weddings, fundraisers and special events.

For more casual visits, the dining room, above, beckons.

when guests enjoyed a leisurely lunch or afternoon tea in 1925, as music drifted down from the Minstrels' Gallery. Today, on Fridays and Saturdays, it's the lounge music of Jose Poniera that floats through the room.

Bel and Albo's determination to provide the decor, comfort, service and amenities found at railroad hotels across Canada ninety years ago extends to other areas of the hotel. On the lower level, where the Factor's Table restaurant was once located, a breakfast room offers light repasts from 8 a.m. to noon. Lunches, dinners and banquets are held in the meeting rooms, including the Provencher and Macdonald Rooms, while the two magnificent ballrooms are places where special events routinely become treasured memories. Not surprisingly, they are booked every weekend.

Once again, the Fort Garry is a place to see and be seen. Recent guests include Rhea Perlman, star of the Cheers television series and James Brolin, in town to direct and act in a film. Prominent visitors from the past have included Sir Laurence Olivier,

Looming above the last remnant of its namesake, the hotel has a timeless quality, year round.

"Midwife" to the CBC

An enthusiastic and confident executive, CNR president Sir Henry Thornton recognized the potential of radio entertainment as a diversion for passengers as they travelled the northern route across the continent. His response in the 1920s was the establishment of the first coast-to-coast radio network in North America, created by installing radio receivers on a number of passenger trains and building radio stations in CNR hotels in major cities along the route. The hotel stations maintained the strong radio signals necessary for widespread program broadcasting.

Thornton insisted on professional hotel orchestras and performers for his pioneering network, and achieved a double whammy of sorts by broadcasting their live performances in front of dinner audiences from roof-top studios in CNR hotels across Canada.

In Ottawa, the radio studios in the Chateau Laurier also aired speeches by politicians and other public figures, who strolled over from Parliament Hill to give their messages directly to the Canadian people. The broadcasts were soon recognized assets for the Chateau Laurier and the Hotel Fort Garry, where Saturday night dinner dances and afternoon tea dances were weekly events.

In this way, CN radio foreshadowed the Canadian Broadcasting Corportation, established in 1936.

There are now five people living at the hotel where Marjorie Eaton resided in 1971 when she was helped down the stairs after a fire broke out.

Nat King Cole, Marcel Marceau and Louis Armstrong.

In short, the Hotel Fort Garry is a place where railway presidents Charles Hayes and Sir Henry Thornton would feel right at home. And they would likely be pleased that the building has been declared a National Historic Site and has Manitoba Heritage status.

Performers, such as Herb Plum and his Orchestra seen here about 1930, played not only for dinner audiences in the hotel, but also for passengers on the company's railways across the country.

May V. Fawley, Provincial Archives of Manitoba / N–9721

Showpiece of a Continent

You can learn a great deal about a country – or a province – by examining its government buildings. Their architectural style usually reflects the mood of the population at the time they were built. Manitoba's Legislative Building is certainly a case in point. An impressive home to politicians and public servants, in 1920 it was acclaimed by architectural experts to be among the grandest government houses in North America. Some say only the American White House in Washington, DC surpasses its beauty and grandeur.

Famous across Canada for its glittering Golden Boy statue, which reaches skyward from a copper-clad dome, the interior of the building is equally familiar to most Manitobans thanks to televised media scrums with the

The dome of Manitoba's present Legislative Building, with its famous statue of the Golden Boy, is perhaps the province's best-known architectural feature.

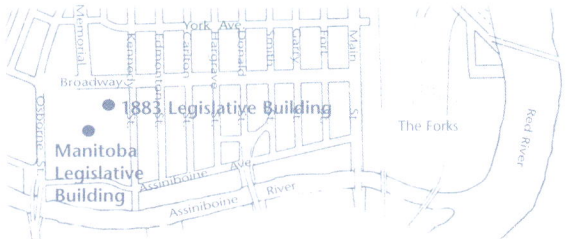

premier and the daily taping of discussion and debate between the government and the opposition during a legislative session.

But film doesn't capture the true beauty of the building's architecture, which speaks of the cultural sentiments of an age when the British Empire was

Its predecessor, built in 1883, was an ornate Italianate design that even in the spring had a brooding quality about it.

Rough Justice

Name calling, heated arguments, even endless fillibusters have never been uncommon in government. But since February 1873, nobody has suffered the kind of rough justice endured by the Manitoba Legislative Assembly's first speaker, Dr. Curtis J. Bird, who was dragged from his sleigh and had hot oil thrown over him for an adverse ruling he had made regarding a bill to incorporate the City of Winnipeg.

Resentment ran high among citizens who had asked for revisions to the bill, including a tax cut. Bird's ruling held up passage of the legislation for incorporation and required the city to establish a council and draw up a system of laws and regulations.

The son of a Hudson's Bay Company factor, Bird had studied medicine in England and was a member of the provisional government called by Louis Riel to draw up a Bill of Rights for the prairies. He also owned a drugstore that contained the first soda fountain in the West.

Bird never fully recovered from his traumatic experience, it seems. He died of pneumonia in London, while on a trip to England with Rupert's Land Archbishop S.P. Matheson.

globally dominant and Greco-Roman design was enjoying a worldwide renaissance.

Over time, the building has lost its image as a grandiose monument to political power and instead gained status as a masterpiece in neo-classical art and sculpture, a place where people can gather to protest or to celebrate.

Visitors by the tens of thousands tour the building's spacious halls, rotundas and reception rooms each year. As citizens of the province, Manitobans – whose taxes to support the government and its programs and policies – have come to view the building as their own personal treasure.

Over the years, they have dropped in to meet their legislators on New Year's Day, sing carols at Christmas and view regular exhibits of work by Manitoba artists. They've held sit-ins in the offices of cabinet ministers or in tents on the legislative lawns. Many stop for coffee in its cafeteria, dine in the Golden Boy restaurant and get TO PAGE 89

Provincial Archives of Manitoba / N–620

Built after Dr. Curtis Bird was attacked, but before Fort Osborne vacated much of the land east of Osborne Street, the province's second legislature faced Kennedy Street. In this 1899 photograph, Government House is at the upper left, and cyclists and a mounted patrol can be seen on Broadway.

By 1910, a building that had once seemed spacious and elegant was beginning to feel cramped and uninspiring. The province, its eyes firmly on the future, wanted something grander and more imposing.

The Architects

Tagged as "a preacher of sermons in stone" for his classic architectural styling, Frank Worthington Simon was fifty years old in 1912, when he submitted his plan to Manitoba. He had designed buildings and supervised construction of the First International Exhibition in Edinburgh, as well as the Cotton Exchange, the Mersey docks and Harbour Board buildings in Liverpool.

Born in Germany in 1862, educated in England and apprenticed to architectural firms in Glasgow, Birmingham and Edinburgh, he had also spent a year in Paris at the Ecole des Beaux-Arts in the 1880s, studying under Jean Louis Pascal, a man recognized for his passion for sixteenth-century Italian Renaissance design.

The winning submission, created by England's Frank Simon in 1912, was both grand and inspiring, a building that would "lift up [Manitobans'] hearts".

An exponent of Victorian values, Simon shared his contemporaries' fascination with ancient cultures and civilizations, social justice and law, courage and discipline. He was determined to give Manitobans, who had "no mountains to lift up their hearts", a chance to raise their eyes skywards above flat prairie vistas. Simon wanted the new building to "make people around it more perceptive, more intelligent, better balanced and altogether more civilized human beings." In newspaper interviews he remarked that "people couldn't be happy or good in surroundings that were commonplace, ugly or uninspiring."

He was extremely sensitive to criticism. When Dr. Charles Gordon, a Winnipeg minister and internationally popular author who wrote under the penname Ralph Connor, told Simon that he thought the Golden Boy was running with the wrong foot forward, Simon took great umbrage.

Gordon's books, which sold by the millions in North America and Europe, extolled the merits of human sacrifice and Christian courage. According to 1920s provincial librarian and newspaper columnist J.W. Healy, Simon told Gordon to "stick to Sky Piloting", a reference to Gordon's fictional hero, the Sky Pilot, who advocated strong personal and family values. Simon said he'd like to see Dr. Gordon running as fast as he could holding a torch in one hand and a wheat sheaf in the crook of his left arm. "Would you change the torch to your left hand every time you put your left foot forward?" he asked.

Henry Boddington the Third, who collaborated with Simon in designing the building, was thirty-one the year that he drafted the plan and shared the competition prize. He later became an associate member of the Royal Institute of Architects. He also served as a director of his family's brewery in Manchester, England, where he designed many of the company's British pubs and reconstructed the brewery itself after it was bombed in World War II.

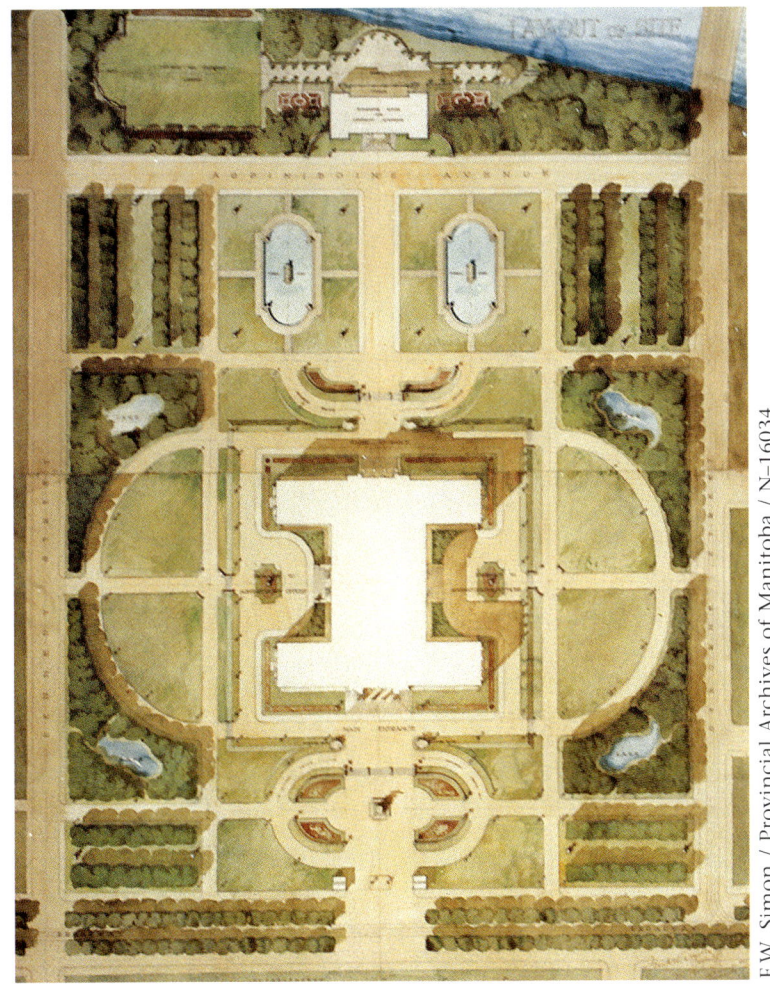

Centred on the land between Osborne and Kennedy, the new legislature would rival any government building in North America.

The realization of Simon's magnificent conception, with its thousands of sculptural and artistic details inside and out, took seven years during a period interrupted by war, labor and materials shortages and spiralling construction costs.

together for family photographs on the beautiful Grand Staircase. Some catch up on what's happening in Manitoba by browsing through provincial community newspapers delivered each week to the second floor Reading Room.

In September 1997, 10,000 men and women lined up in the building to sign the book of condolences following the death of Diana, Princess of Wales. On rare occasions they've come to dance on the same marble floors that Members of the Legislative Assembly and their spouses waltzed around when the building opened in 1920, an event recreated by the Winnipeg Symphony Women's Committee in 1967.

A decade of progress and prosperity at the turn of the twentieth century gave Manitoba's elected politicians the heady impetus to commence the building of a handsome new Legislative Building in 1911.

As the gateway to the west in the early 1900s, Winnipeg was a boomtown: the centre of Canada's transportation system. In 1910 it was a mecca for land developers, bankers, grain speculators, merchants and hordes of immigrants eager to work hard to build a new life in a new country.

As well, Winnipeg's population had exploded to 151,958 from 700 in the forty-one years since the original postage-stamp shaped territory gained provincial status in 1870.

Buoyed by optimism and confidence in a province in which three million people were expected to reside by the year 2000, legislators fancied an imposing capital building with space for increased government business. They wanted a building "not for present delight or use alone, but such as our descendants will thank us for". What better way to bolster expectations for

(left and right): Peter St. John; (centre): Dennis Fast

Above the main entrance is a sculptured frieze, (left and right) that tells the settlement story of Manitoba. Inside (centre), a marble balustrade outside the Legislative Chamber surrounds a portal for viewing the Pool of the Black Star below.

future wealth and success than to build an impressive building?

Not only did they want a building infinitely more imposing than TO PAGE 91

The Golden Boy

Glittering in the sun by day, his lighted torch a beacon by night, the Golden Boy atop Manitoba's Legislative Building is the province's best known symbol, bearing a message of eternal youth and enterprise.

Commissioned in 1911 and created by Parisian sculptor Georges Gardet, the goldleaf-covered statue soars seventy-three-metres above the ground. His eyes look north to the province's wealth in mineral resources, lumber, furs, fish and water power, as well as its Arctic seaport. At the time he was commissioned, it was assumed that Manitoba, with its mid-continent port and long history as a transportation hub, would soon be home to millions of people. The opening of the Panama Canal in 1914, which eliminated the long and dangerous circumnavigation of North America's southern tip, changed that prognosis. But Manitoba's rich resources remain.

The statue weighs five tonnes and stands 4.9 metres from toe to torch, where a mercury vapor lamp was installed on December 31st, 1966 to mark Canada's Centennial.

The Golden Boy is a runner, akin to Hermes the messenger in Greek mythology. He carries a sheaf of golden grain in tribute to Manitoba's agricultural industry in his left arm. In his right hand he holds high a torch to lead Manitobans in a race to the future. The Golden Boy is also a survivor. Before installation, he survived a German army shelling of the French foundry in Barbidienne, where he was cast in 1917. Then, loaded aboard the *Empress of France* for his voyage to Canada, he found himself press-ganged into war service. Just prior to sailing, the ship was commandeered by the Allied forces and for the balance of the war was used to transport troops and munitions across the Atlantic and through Mediterranean waters patrolled by torpedo-laden German submarines. Lying prone in the hold, the Golden Boy served as ballast.

Not until 1919 was he finally unloaded in Halifax for the journey to Winnipeg. Typically, he arrived just in time. Hoisted to the top of the new dome in November 1919, he glistened in the sun as the building was officially opened on July 15th, 1920.

Since early 2001, the Golden Boy has been undergoing a much needed refurbishment behind an acrylic, glass and aluminum frame scaffolding. During this process, it was discovered that the armature supporting the statue had been corroded. The decision on repairs were made following a series of tests that simulated the effects of wind and ice at the University of Western Ontario. The tests used information obtained from three dimensional digital photogrammetry done at the Legislative Building site.

Peter St. John

Another problem concerned the statue's shimmering golden skin. After considering other alternatives aimed at protecting the bronze casting from the effects of pollution, it was decided to reapply 24-carat gold leaf, originally plated in 1951. The restoration and the scaffolding around the statue have allowed rare closeup views and photographs of a boy most people see only from more than 100 metres away. He is, according to *Winnipeg Free Press* editorial writer Gerald Flood, who visited last spring, "a beautiful boy, with long, layered hair, a cupid's mouth and a fine chin."

Beautifully muscled and anatomically correct, he appears just as nature intended and is, as Gardet undoubtedly envisioned nearly a century ago, a timeless figure linking the classical past to the twenty-first century and beyond.

When the renovations are complete, the Golden Boy's torch will be lit by a fixture that does not require the regular replacement of bulbs, a precarious job that has for decades required maintenance workers to scale the dome and the statue aided by nothing more than ladders they carried with them.

Corinthian columns soar skyward, leading the eye to the nimble figure above.

Peter St. John

the rough-hewn log house at Main Street and McDermot Avenue acquired from landowner and businessman A.G.B. Bannatyne, which served as a provincial capital building soon after Manitoba joined Confederation in 1870. They also rejected any idea of expanding the existing beige brick Italianate-style Legislative Building, which faced Kennedy Street. By 1913, new and grand was the only way to go. Unfortunately, neither the original $2.5 million estimated cost of a new building nor the population growth lived up to expectations.

As the good times continued, a Conservative government under Sir Rodmond Roblin advertised in 1911 for architectural plans from "subjects of the British Empire only". The building was to be erected on the site of the Fort Osborne Barracks non-commissioned officers' married quarters. The province purchased the property from the federal government for $200,000 in 1912, with a proviso that the quarters would be demolished immediately.

The competition attracted sixty-seven entries from British and Canadian architects vying for the $10,000 prize plus the $100,000 commission. Liverpool architect Frank Worthington Simon of the British partnership

The Artists

Internationally famous sculptors, carvers and artists were selected by Frank Simon to produce major works for the building. They included Parisian sculptor Georges Gardet, who prepared the models of Moses and Solon, the two bison on the Grand Staircase and the model and casting of the statue of the Golden Boy for a total fee of $13,761. Solon, Moses and the bison were cast in bronze by the Roman Bronze Works in Brooklyn, New York.

There's an intriguing tale occasionally told by tour guides about how the two huge bronze bison were conveyed across an ice covered marble floor to their massive pedestals before being hoisted in place in 1919. Provincial archivists claim the story is totally untrue, but it does add a nice touch of whimsy for visitors on a tour of this extraordinary building.

It's probable the story originated from a passage in *Terror In Winnipeg*, a novel for teens written by Canadian author Eric Wilson. In the story, Wilson has a teacher

A pair of massive bronze bison, symbols of Manitoba, guard the main staircase.

Showpiece of a Continent

challenge students touring the legislature with the question: "How did the builders get such heavy (bison) statues across the marble floor without scratching it?" When no one in the class can answer he tells them: "They put them on big chunks of ice and slid them across the floor."

His explanation goes on to claim the ice was made by flooding the marble floor, then opening the entry doors in sub-zero January weather. Once the bison were in place the doors were closed and the ice quickly melted. It's not explained how all that water was mopped up.

Providing some background for Wilson's tale is the way that four seven-tonne statues of early adventurers were installed on the exterior staircases. They were actually hoisted onto blocks of ice during installation at the east and west porticos in July 1920 and then sank into place as the ice melted in the heat of the day.

Albert Hodge, of London, prepared models of the pediment, the sphinxes, the caryatides and the figures above the east and west door pediments for $10,463, while Bernie Rhind, a Scot, prepared plaster models of the four groups of statues at the base of the dome for $5,510. F.A. Purdy of Chicago carved Rhind's models and Hodge's sphinx in stone on site, charging just over $9,000. New York's Piccirilli Brothers carved in stone the caryatides, the front, east and west pediments and the statues of La Vérendrye, Selkirk, Wolfe and Dufferin for a total of $49,027.

Albert Hodge of London modelled the pediment frieze (above) and sphinxes, while the carving was done by the Piccirilli Brothers of New York and F.A. Purdy of Chicago.

Augustus Tack of New York painted the mural in the Legislative Chamber with assistance from Winnipeg artist Lemoine Fitzgerald for $33,181, while Sir Frank Brangwyn of England created the war mural over the door of the chamber for $10,104.

The Next-of-Kin Memorial is the work of Winnipeg sculptor Marguerite Taylor and architect Colonel J. N. Siemens.

This rendering of the interior of the Legislative Chamber (left), created by Frank Simon as part of his winning submission, shows the extraordinary detail in his conception. The beauty of the chamber today (right) continues to reflect his vision.

Simon and Boddington was selected in September 1912 by Leonard A. Stokes, president of the Royal Institute of Architects. Though not Canadian, it was deemed that Simon had best expressed the strengths and vitality of Manitoba at the turn of the century. His design called for a neo-classical building with a Greek temple dome and Roman pillar characteristics, popular in North American architecture at the time.

The building's construction was considerably less glorious. It survived materials and labor shortages brought on by the demands of the First World War, as well as turbulent delays created by labor strife, scandal, corruption and a 1919 depression. But when finally

completed, it fulfilled the dreams of the Edwardian era for the future of the province. And almost a century later it continues to meet Simon's goal to inspire Manitobans, and instill in them an ongoing feeling of pride.

The estimated cost of the new building, to be completed within two years, was two million dollars. That price soared to $9,379,000 on completion in 1920, plus an additional $13,726,569 of debt on the interest created TO PAGE 100

These drawings of the "old Leg" (left) and the new one (below) are a visual statement of Manitoba's passage from the nineteenth century into the twentieth. Dreams were larger and visions bolder; only truly classical architecture could express these sentiments in a manner that embraced the future.

Scandal

Scandal rocked the legislature in 1915, when Premier Sir Rodmond P. Roblin's Conservative Party came under the scrutiny of a Royal Commission. At issue were the spiralling costs of construction of the new Legislative Building. From initial estimates of $2.5 million in 1913 and $5 million by 1914, construction costs soared to $9 million plus additional interest on loans by 1920 when the building was completed.

Rumors of faulty construction (reinforced concrete caissons were not sunk deep enough and had to be replaced by steel pilings) and misappropriated government funds inflamed the public in the spring of 1915. Charges raged over overbilling on labor and materials by building contractor Thomas J. Kelly.

Roblin resigned on May 13th 1915 under pressure from the press and his Liberal party opponents and amid labor unrest.

Long before the building was completed, the lawns seeded or the trees planted, the project was beset by controversy.

Kelly's refusal to produce essential billing documents for the Royal Commission added further confusion to the investigation. While Roblin accepted "constitutional responsibility" for the acts of government officials, he was never accused of being party to any dishonesty.

In 1915, a Royal Commission enquiry was appointed to investigate corruption charges against Kelly and Sons for skimming more than $800,000 in billings submitted to the government by Thomas J. Kelly's construction firm.

Kelly fled to the United States, but was extradited and went to trial in June 1916. There, he was proven guilty of an estimated theft of $1.2 million in overbilling. He was sentenced to a two-and-a-half year term in Stony Mountain penitentiary, where he lived in the warden's house.

In 1922, twenty-one parcels of land he owned were confiscated by the Crown to settle the debt. Though rumours circulated for decades that Kelly's Edwardian mansion on Carlton Street had been built with misappropriated funds, in fact it was built in 1907, five years before he won the contract for the legislature. It was among the properties confiscated. His brother Michael's family home on Adelaide Street was also appropriated to pay off the debt. Most reports indicate that about $30,000 of the million-plus debt was recovered by 1941, when it was written down to a nominal evaluation of $25,000. However, in *Substantial Justice: Law and Lawyers in Manitoba – 1670 to 1970*, Dale and Lee Gibson write that $100,000 was eventually repaid.

The seven classic columns that flanked the entrance to Kelly's Edwardian mansion survive today as the entrance to Kelly House, a modern apartment on the site.

Kelly and his brothers, all born in Ireland, had been leaders in local improvement projects in Winnipeg since the 1890s. They were contractors for the first sewers, roads and sidewalks in Winnipeg. Later they completed work on the St. Andrew's locks and dam, a portion of the Shoal Lake aquaduct, the Agricultural College on the Fort Garry campus, the *Manitoba Free Press* building on Carlton Street, the Grain Exchange Building and Canadian National Railway shops in Winnipeg, as well as the Portage Avenue post office and a hotel in Brandon.

Kelly left Winnipeg in 1923 to live in the United States where he worked on major contracts in Kansas, Missouri and Oklahoma. He died in Beverly Hills, California, in 1939 where it is said investments in oil and gas provided him with millions more and allowed him to build another mansion.

Today, Kelly House, a seven-storey apartment block of 120 suites stands on the Carlton Street site of the home Thomas built for his family of eight children. Seven ionic pillars which originally fronted his opulent Edwardian residence remain guarding the apartment building entrance.

Between 1923 and 1970, when the Kelly House apartment complex was built, Kelly's original house served as an RCMP barracks, a boarding house, a residential hotel called Graystone Arms, a dining room hotel called Llentrad Harbour and finally as Kelly House Square, a dining room and motor hotel.

Canadian Department of the Interior / National Archives of Canada / PA-47835

Lit against the night sky and reflected in the river, the finished masterpiece transcends time and place.

by the manner in which the cost of construction, furnishings and grounds landscaping was financed.

By 1954, when the debt was finally retired, the province's imposing capital building had cost more than ten times the initial estimate: $23,105,569. By the time the project was completed and the two architects left Winnipeg, Simon and Boddington's commission, according to the Public Building Report of 1919 totalled $250,000 – as required by their 1912 contract.

The present replacement value of the Manitoba legislature is more than one billion dollars, 500 times the first estimate. In fact, the building should probably be deemed priceless, for should anything happen to it, it could never be replaced. Not only is the cost of materials all but prohibitive, the skilled stonemasons and artisans of ninety years ago are no longer available.

The tenfold increase in financing the cost of the building loomed almost from the day the sod was turned in August 1913. A barrage of unexpected events at home and abroad created shortages of both labor and materials and there were charges of fraudulence and corruption. With the outbreak of World War I in August 1914, thousands of men left the Manitoba workforce to fight overseas. Demand for munitions created both a price increase and a shortage of the steel required for construction. And scandal dogged the government for the next two years over faulty construction and increasing construction costs.

Constructed of Tyndall limestone quarried at Garson, twenty-five miles northwest of Winnipeg, the Legislative Building is built in an H-design. It faces Broadway, immediately south of downtown Winnipeg, and lies in the centre of twelve hectares of landscaped grounds planted with both native and imported shrubs and trees. In the summer, the walkways and rolling lawns are accented by formal flower beds. The gardens are planted annually with 4,000 geraniums, lilies and chrysthanthemums, plus hundreds of petunias, snapdragons and salvia grown in a greenhouse on the riverbank at Kennedy Street.

The Assiniboine River, long a highway for the region's original peoples, as well as for later trappers and traders, forms the southern boundary of the property, while Osborne and Kennedy Streets bound it on the west and east.

Its three floors contain an area of approximately one-quarter of a million square feet or 22,500 square metres. Its two wings, which form the vertical

Summer and winter, the riverside gardens and black lamp standards create a sculptured effect on the south Legislative Grounds.

101

lines of the H are each 328 feet or ninety-eight metres long.

The Tyndall stone is reminiscent of Manitoba's earliest beginnings, when much of the province was covered by a warm sea, much like today's which the Legislative Building stone was stripped. She describes the stone as coming in two colors – "a light buff mixed with brown and a pale gray with darker mottles" which create a "lacy look". Random fossils – gastropods, can now be seen in both interior and exterior walls of the Legislative Building.

The building's art relies on Greek and Roman mythological icons which relate to justice and the law. Pompeian characteristics appear in the textured

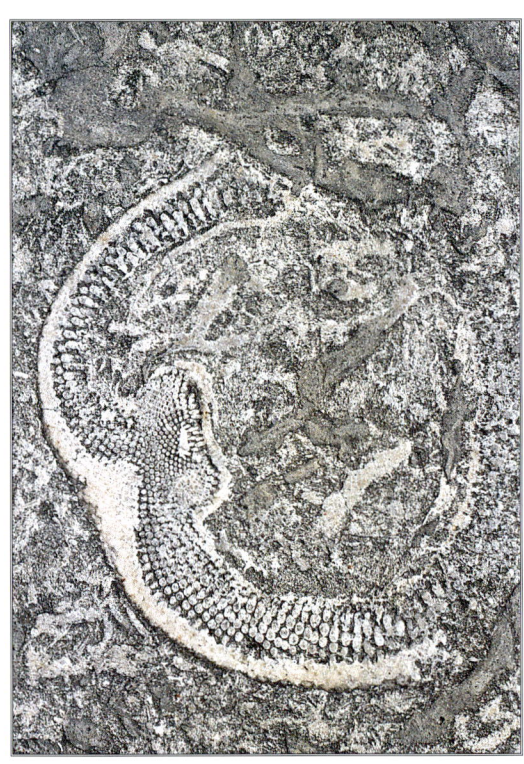

Caribbean (though inhabited by very different creatures). Pulitzer Prize winning author Carol Shields opens *The Stone Diaries* in Tyndall, a town two miles from the Garson quarry from brachiopods, trilobites, corals and snails – were created, writes Shields, "as the flesh of these once living creatures decayed and a limey mud filled the casings and hardened to rock". Such fossils stone walls indoors and outdoors.

One almost has to stand back on Broadway to view the many elements of the legislature's typical temple motif, with its towering pillars and pediments preferred by ancient Greek builders. As they did in ancient Greece, here too they present a bold but simple unity of design.

The wood and brass enclosed front entry faces north and is reached by climbing twenty steps of granite.

Manitoba's economic and agricultural growth as Canada's keystone province.

The stone carvings depict Canada's motto – "From Sea to Sea" – with a nautical wheel (for the Atlantic provinces) at the east end and a trident (for the

Above the doorway is a massive pediment – a sculptured frieze – set between the roof and the bottom of six towering ionic pillars. Carvings along its length allegorically relate the story of

Pacific coast) at the west end. A series of carved figures stretching across the pediment represents European immigration, productive farming and a young family in a new land. The seated

From the Tyndall limestone (far left), with its fossilized remnants of a much earlier era, the sculptors created columns, cornices, pillars and pediments that echoed the classical art of the

Mediterranean. The exterior sculpture, including this modern representation of Louis Riel (above), presents larger-than-life figures from several of Manitoba's constituent cultures.

The Grand Staircase, with its three tiers of Carrera marble stairs, leads visitors up to the Legislative Chamber, the heart of the building. Those who gather here prior to taking tours of the building rarely fail to be awed by the beauty and scale of this grand entrance. Seasonal displays of flowers and greenery add to the spectacle.

figure at centre is a sculptor's vision of Manitoba. Two sphinx-like statues lie just above the pediment at east and west corners. Replicas of figures from Egyptian mythology, each has the body of a lion and the head of the reigning pharaoh. The sphinx of Greek myth killed anyone who could not answer its riddle.

Set on the four corners of the building are four groups of statues representing provincial enterprise in agriculture, art, industry and science.

Two more groups of statues, each sitting on a stone chest, can be found above uncarved pediments over the east and west doors. On the west the figures represent peace; to the east, helmeted figures depict war.

Inside, the symmetry and mythical symbolism of Simon and Boddington's neo-classical plan is dazzling. An imposing formal entry hall leads to the six-metre-wide Carrera marble Grand Staircase contained within marble handrails. The rotunda floor of black Vermont marble and antique verde marble, combined with pink polished Tennessee marble provides an excellent contrast to the Legislative Building's quarried stone walls. The broad marble stairs rise in three tiers of thirteen steps to form a courtyard approach to the Assembly Chamber.

According to Greek allegory, though thirteen was an unlucky number, its demonic force could be nullified through repeated use. Simon applied the theory dramatically, installing thirteen global lights along all long hallways, and thirteen carved circles around the door frame to the Legislative Chamber.

At the base of the stairs, shifting patterns of light filter down from a rectangular skylight onto two massive North American bison cast in Herculean bronze with a patina finish. Their 2.5-tonne bodies are reflected in the polished marble floors.

The surrounding stone walls are defined by columns, statues and carvings. Gazing down from opposite walls above the bison are the heads of Minerva (the goddess of wisdom) and Medusa (the gorgon with snakes for hair, whose staring eyes could turn a person to stone). A carved stone copy of sculptured female caryatides, which echoes the Porch of the Maidens in the Erechtheum in Athens, rises up to support the third-floor level.

Modelled in plaster, oxen skulls edge the skylight in the Grand Staircase area. Simon meant them to be reminders of the skeletal heads of cattle customarily sacrificed in ancient religious ceremonies, not replicas of the bleached bison bones left on western prairies, though the latter might have been a more appropriate interpretation.

Centred on the arches that open onto the east and west hallways are lions' heads, the fabled symbols of courage. Behind the Grand Staircase lies the Pool of the Black Star, an enigmatic eight-pointed marble star centered exactly at the basal axis of the building's main floor.

Sixteen columns set around a base of three steps of the star area provide a perfect space for the art exhibits which have been held here, although the star is actually a version of a "cell" or "vault" upon which ancient Greeks offered sacrifices.

A similar space in the Saskatchewan Legislative Building in Regina is modelled after Napoleon's tomb in Les Invalides in Paris. In Alberta's capital building in Edmonton, a fountain serves as the cell.

At the top of the Grand Staircase, an eight-metre circular antechamber features a floor of polished Tennessee and Vermont marble edged with a continuous Greek key design in verde antique marble, an ancient symbol of the eternal quest for knowledge. Overhead, the inner great dome rises

Winter Proof

The exterior sculptures took more than artistic imagination to create. They also required a knowledge of Manitoba's climate and its effects on stone. This photograph shows the top of the head of the central figure in the Industry statue on the northwest corner at the base of the dome. The piece being held was added to the main block to allow more material to carve. Rather than attaching it permanently, however, it was joined to the main figure with a tenon and mortise, allowing water in the joint to freeze and thaw without breaking the surrounding stone.

Courtesy of Legislative Building / Winnipeg 2001

Light from the glass "eye" illuminates the entry to the Legislative Chamber.

to a stippled-glass eye. From this eye light filters down on a dramatic seven-by five-metre war mural set above the doors to the Legislative Chamber. The mural was painted by Sir Frank Brangwyn of London to interpret the tragedy and sacrifice the men of World War I endured in fighting the "war to end all wars".

Additional illumination into this area comes from four small windows, which allow daylight to filter down on the blue and ivory plaster wedges set between four twelve-metre steel ribs.

A circular Italian marble balustrade centered in this rotunda allows visitors to look down on the mystic Pool of the Black Star below. Although the star may look off-centre, it's an optical illusion. The opening is actually directly above the star and the balustrade circumference is the same size as the circle around the star.

Inside, the Legislative Chamber, the only one in Canada in which members' benches are grouped in a horseshoe-style semicircle, is furnished in blue and ivory. This Legislative Assembly is home to a unicameral system of government, a single legislative body elected by fifty-seven electoral divisions in the province. Greater Winnipeg MLAs number thirty-two.

When it opened in 1920, the building was the seat of both legislative and administrative departments of the provincial government. It now houses only the ministers of the provincial cabinet, their deputies and ministerial staff. The sixty desks and chairs of hand-carved walnut, inlaid with ebony, are arranged in three tiers rising from a blue-carpeted sunken floor in the Legislative Chamber. Matching blue leather covers the chair seats.

The chamber walls are painted light ivory, their niches covered with matching broadloom (to improve acoustics), then draped in matching velvet curtains. In 1920, a noted Chicago architect said the chamber's inexpensive (in his view) furnishings and restful decor was part of the room's charm in contrast to overfurnished rooms in other capitol buildings.

Protocol dating back to the earliest of British Parliaments in the thirteenth century dicatates the seating arrangement in all Canadian legislatures, as well as in the House of Commons in Ottawa. Government members sit to the

The polished marble floor of the rotunda gleams in the filtered light. Visitors often remark on how beautifully the Legislative Building is maintained.

Above the speaker's chair (inset), a mural by A.V. Tack portrays Justice surrounded by humanity in all its strengths and frailties. Below it are the names of some of the world's great lawmakers.

right of the speaker; opposition party and independent members to the left.

Above and behind the speaker is the press gallery, with seating for thirteen. The public gallery, which seats 200, encircles the remaining wall recess above the chamber floor. The public gallery is open whenever the assembly is in session, except on opening day when attendance is by invitation only.

A television camera is housed behind blue curtains behind the speaker's chair to record MLAs in debate. Another TV camera is mounted beside the main north door to tape the speaker. Messenger rooms are located to the right and left of the speaker with the left room also used by translators required to interpret proceedings during Question Period.

The clerk of the Legislative Assembly, deputy clerk and clerk assistant sit just below the speaker at a long table in the center of the horseshoe, with the sergeant-at-arms seated facing the clerk of the Legislative Assembly Each desk is equipped with a microphone connected to a public address system and a recording machine. The latter is used in the publication of *Hansard*, a verbatim report of debates and proceedings in the house. Named after Luke Hansard, the first printer in the British House of Commons, this printed record of everything said in legislature debates and Question Period is transcribed from the tapes into a computer and then edited to eliminate only false starts, aahs, umms and gibberish. Heckling and heated argument are integrated into *Hansard* and a printout of each day's edited transcript is sent to each member, with a three-hour time limit on corrections. Any changes made must not alter or censor the meaning of the transcript. When corrections are made, French is translated into English and English into French for the Queen's printer. The finished version is delivered the following day to each member's desk.

Newspapers and libraries subscribe to *Hansard*, allowing voters to read exactly what was said by their politicians.

All art in the Legislative Chamber bolsters the theme of legislated justice from antiquity to the present. Written in Latin on a panel above a mural painted by American artist Augustus Vincent Tack is *Si quid patrimini propter Justitian beati*, which translates as "Blessed are you who suffer anything for the sake of Justice".

Tack's allegorical murals, which are inset above and behind the speaker's chair, present an image of Justice flanked by two handmaidens and a group of figures who represent the young and old, rich and poor, strong and weak of the world. Side murals display images of Mercy and Faith, Hope and Charity.

Elsewhere on the second floor, Rooms 254 and 255, located at either side of the south wall of the building, serve as both committee or reception rooms, depending on the occasion. Brown Carrera marble, with carved olive leaves, frame the entry doors and baseboards to both seven- by twenty-eight-metre rooms, which are panelled in walnut to a height of one metre. In Room 255, the drapes are purple and the carpeting is blue. Room 254 has brown drapes and carpets.

Oil portraits (all by V.A. Long) of the first nine premiers from Alfred Boyd to Hugh John Macdonald line the walls of Room 254. Portraits of the next ten premiers, from Sir Rodmond P. Roblin to Howard Pawley hang in Room 255.

Visiting royalty and foreign dignitaries are always received by Manitoba's lieutenant governor in Room 235, a formal reception room in the east wing that is panelled in black American walnut inlaid with ebony. An adjoining room serves as an office where the lieutenant governor signs orders in council. Hand-carved designs decorate the ceiling and four corner pillars of the room.

Street of Dreams: The Story of Broadway

The lieutenant governor receives visiting royalty or heads of state here, in the Reception Salon. The beautiful room features black walnut panelling and a mahogany desk.

The walnut entry door is framed in brown Carrera marble with overlapping olive leaves carved on the surface. The carpet was handwoven in Donegal, Ireland.

To the right of the lieutenant governor's mahogany desk sits the Prince of Wales chair reserved for visiting British royalty. First used in Saint John, New Brunswick in 1860 by Edward VII when he was Prince of Wales, the chair carries the official royal coat-of-arms on the back. It was brought west from New Brunswick by a soldier transferred to the Red River settlement. Brass medallions along the back of the chair display the names of royals who have visited the room since 1901, from George, Prince of Cornwall and York (who later became King George V) to Charles, Prince of Wales, who visited the city for a second time in 1996.

Names engraved on the medallions include: Edward Albert, Prince of Wales who later became Edward VII (1860); George, Duke of Cornwall and York, who became George V (1901); Edward, Prince of Wales (familiarly known as David), who became Edward VIII before abdicating the throne in 1936 (1919); George VI (1939); Princess Elizabeth in 1951, later to return to Winnipeg as Elizabeth II with her consort,

Prince Philip, in 1984; Princess Margaret (1971); Charles, Prince of Wales (1975 and 1996); Princess Anne (1982); Prince Andrew, Duke of York (1987); Prince Edward (1990).

Formal photographs of twentieth-century British sovereigns who have visited Manitoba hang on the walls. A guest book, which sits open on the desk, is replaced about every ten months when all the pages are filled with signatures.

Located at Room 200 in the north front wing is the very large (seven metres by thirty metres) Manitoba Room. This is the scene of formal government gatherings and dinners for royalty or visiting provincial premiers. Citizenship ceremonies for new Canadians and the Order of Manitoba awards are also held here.

Brass medallions on the Prince of Wales chair (left) mark the visits of each heir to the British throne since 1901. Tiny bison cap the hardware on the walnut entry doors (centre), and below, beautifully carved black American walnut cornices and panels decorate the pillars and the ceiling, lending the Reception Room a warm ambience.

The vaulted ceiling rises two storeys, ionic columns divide the main portion of the room, which is lit by three brass and crystal chandeliers.

A portrait of King George V is flanked by ionic columns in the Manitoba or Speaker's Reception Room.

The room is decorated in ivory, green and blue, the colors of Manitoba's coat of arms.

Oil paintings of the late George V and Queen Mary (by V.A. Long) and of Elizabeth II and Prince Philip (by royal portraitist Denis Fieldes in London) hang from the walls. A close look at the latter portraits reveals a bit of artistic magic, for viewers have the sense that the queen and her husband are constantly keeping an eye on visitors to the room.

A glass case below the centre window houses replicas of the four Books of Remembrance on display in the Peace Tower in Ottawa. The books contain the names of 114,710 names of Canadian war dead with a separate book listing the names of 1,500 merchant marine casualties during World War II, including eight women. Two hundred eighty-three Canadians died in the Boer War in South Africa and the Nile expedition. There were 66,655 casualties in World War I, 44,893 in World War II and 516 in the Korean War. Every morning a page in each book is turned so that every name is displayed at least once a year.

The Reading Room, number 260 in the south wing, has two mezzanine galleries, their shelved alcoves stacked with thousands of books of reference, magazines and provincial newspapers. Stairs and an elevator provide entry to the second and third level of books where copies of *Hansard* (dating back to 1958) are housed beneath a blue, red and gold coffered ceiling. On a final inspection tour of the building in 1920, Simon requested removal of all volumes of Manitoba Blue Bills, recording the first reading of bills in the legislature. The color of their bindings was not to his taste; he believed it clashed with the room decor. His request was rejected.

Walnut furniture, upholstered in muted crimson leather, blend with the red, buff and blue bindings of the books used by students, writers, journalists and researchers seeking current and historical information.

Seven plaster of Paris mini-statues of Canadian parliamentarians and a French-Canadian clergyman who contributed to Manitoba's early history stand on a carved walnut newspaper file cabinet beneath the south windows.

Carved in in 1886 by seventy-seven-year-old Quebec sculptor Louis Phillipe Hèbert the figures show Sir Étienne-Paschal Taché, Sir Hector Langevin, Sir Louis-Hippolyte Lafontaine, Sir George-Étienne Cartier, Augustin Norbert Morin, Père Labelle and Sir John A. Macdonald posed in debate. A bronze bust of Sir John A. Macdonald, Canada's first prime minister, stands in the corner to the right of the entry.

The premier's office (Room 204), the Cabinet Room, caucus rooms (227 and 234) and the Members' Lounge (Room 236) are all located on the second floor, but are off limits for casual visitors.

For the best view of the building's magnificent interior, head for the third floor. Here, looking down from the bridge over the rotunda to the Pool of the Black Star, the building's grandeur and beauty, as well as the architect's vision, are immediately evident. Eight government ministers, their deputies and office staff have offices of the third floor.

Above is the tower, which is empty except for space between the inner and outer dome where the building's mechanical equipment is housed. A twisting stairway leads to a hatch door that opens beneath the Golden Boy, allowing inspection and repairs.

Down on the lowest or basement level are offices for maintenance, management and security personnel, as well as four public washrooms, two for men and two for women. A security staff is on duty twenty-four hours a day, 365 days a year. Extra security personnel is brought in on special occasions such as the Manitoba 125 fireworks demonstration in 1995, when 60,000 people gathered on the Legislative Grounds to watch the spectacle.

Four stairways, rising from basement to the third floor, are located at each corner of the building with two staircases in the centre. Elevators operate at the northwest and southeast corners of the building.

There is no furnace in the building. Heat comes from a central power house on Memorial Boulevard, through pipes tunnelled under Broadway. The power house also heats eight other buildings: the new and old Law Courts, the Land Titles building, the Woodsworth Building, the Remand Centre, the Provincial Archives building, the Norquay Building and the trade shop at 444 Vaughan Street.

A vacuum system, the first to be installed in a government building in Canada, is still in place, but now requires regular repairs.

Several incumbents of the premier's office, the heart of political power in Manitoba, have had a lasting impact on the nation as a whole. The office includes a fireplace that, bowing to the priceless nature of the building, is no longer used.

Palace of Justice

Nothing demonstrates architectural change in Winnipeg over a period of ninety years better than a look at the Law Courts and Land Titles buildings on Broadway. Both symbolize the wealth and power of the state in their neoclassical design and Tyndall stone structure. Together, they complement the impressive Legislative Building to form an enclave of government business. And with their modern counterparts along and across Kennedy Street, they demonstrate how public buildings have changed in the past century.

On its completion in 1916, the court house met newly established government requirements that materials and talent in their construction be Canadian, and was acclaimed as "one of the finest provincial complexes in Canada".

Department of the Interior / National Archives of Canada / detail of PA-47878

The entrance to the present Law Courts at the corner of Broadway and Kennedy.

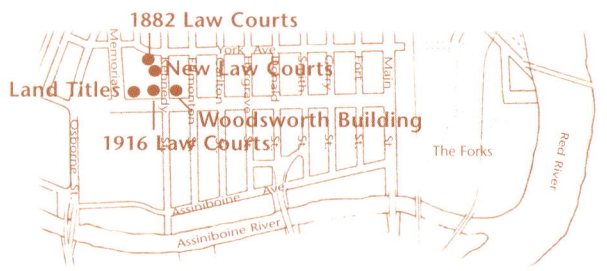

Palace of Justice

This new building, which replaced the 1882 Law Courts on Broadway at Kennedy, was the fifth in a succession of court houses in what had become the eastern judicial district. Its predecessors, some of which were combined with jails, dated back to 1830 in the Red River community. TO PAGE 117

The 1882 Law Courts, a rather ornate Victorian structure, was located on Kennedy Street at York Avenue. In 1894 the building was expanded to include the wing on the right of the painting.

99 - Court House, Winnipeg.

M.I. Guthrie / Provincial Archives of Manitoba

The Land Titles Building

Manitoba's old Land Titles office at 393 Broadway has the solid stone construction found in government buildings across Canada and the United States at the beginning of the twentieth century. Located at the corner of Kennedy Street and Broadway just west of the 1916 Law Courts, it was built by the Manitoba government in 1903 at a cost of $83,000 from a design by provincial architect Samuel Hooper.

Three storeys high, with marble columns, marble floors and rectangular lintels over the front and side windows, it was a repository of the province's land titles records for nearly eighty-five years. Particularly in the early decades, the building was often a busy, hectic place. This was where newcomers went to register land purchases, search for liens on property or sign legal documents for conveying real estate or transfering deeds.

In 1987, it took on a new role following a two million dollar conversion into chambers for Court of Appeal and Queen's Bench judges, including the chief justice and associate justice. Twenty-six rooms were updated to become spacious and elegantly furnished offices.

A heritage stained glass window centred by the Manitoba bison emblem floods light into a landing between the first and second floors. And paintings by Canadian artists, the majority of them Manitobans, line the walls on all three floors.

Connected to the Law Courts Building by an elevated corridor, a robing room in the lower level was created to store the robes judges don for court appearances.

The Land Titles Building was one of the busiest places in Manitoba in the first years after it opened.

Palace of Justice

Providing an eye-catching contrast, the $20 million Woodsworth Building (at the southwest corner of Kennedy and Broadway), with its second-storey walkway to the 1916 Law Courts, is a modern glass and metal structure. It offers a more relaxed architectural interpretation and includes an addition that serves as the Small Claims Court. Named for social advocate James S. Woodsworth, founder of the CCF, the Cooperative Commonwealth Federation (forerunner of today's New Democratic Party or NDP), the building opened in 1987. The total cost was twenty times more than the 1916 Law Courts next door.

However, in the same year, the Law Courts got a $12 million facelift, expanding the number of court rooms from eighteen to thirty. The Land Titles Building, on a site adjacent to the court house was converted into judges chambers at a cost of $2.5 million, forming an intregated complex on Broadway.

The very first court house in Red River was also on Broadway, though the street was unmarked and unnamed at the time. It stood just inside Upper Fort Garry, a visible symbol of the legal authority the Hudson's Bay Company had undertaken in Rupert's Land, to regulate, among other things, the use of fire, trespassing animals and horse theft. In 1836, the sale of liquor to the Cree, Assiniboine and other aboriginal peoples was prohibited. Informants who reported such offences were awarded a share of the fine.

The first court house and jail, located inside the walls of Upper Fort Garry, were simpler structures.

In 1844, the court house and jail were moved outside the walls of Upper Fort Garry to a tiny wooden structure located near its southeast bastion. The company had decided it was "exceedingly dangerous to have the public jails within its walls". The settlers, however, saw it as an attempt on the part of the HBC to disassociate itself from the administration of justice, at least in the public mind.

After the company rejected the city's request to lease one of the fort's bastions for a jail in 1873, the fledgling Manitoba government authorized construction of a combined courthouse and jail at a cost of something under $40,000.

This third court house was a strange architectural mix: oak log walls covered in pine siding, rectangular windows, exterior stairways, a jail and many chimneys. It opened in 1874 on the west side of Main Street between Bannatyne and William and for the next eight years served many purposes, among them a meeting place for the Legislative Assembly and space for charity bazaars.

By 1882, it was replaced by a more dignified $200,000 Victorian-style

From Substantial Justice: Law and Lawyers in Manitoba, 1670 – 1970. Courtesy of Lee Gibson

117

structure on Kennedy Street between York and Broadway. A red brick and sandstone structure, four storeys high with a mansard roof and a tower, it had well-lighted court rooms and modern conveniences including steam heating.

This fourth Law Courts Building, built on "Old Driveway Park", was essential to the handling of an expanded judicial system. The decision to build county court houses, land registry offices and jails in each of the five Manitoba counties necessitated an allocation of $5,000 for each authorized county to impose local levies to pay for the buildings. In Winnipeg, a system of stamps for every legal conveyance, such as the sale of property, was contemplated to offset the building costs. However, this excise tax was delayed for two years.

Within ten years, the red brick court house was busy beyond its capacity, with trials frequently postponed because all the court rooms were in use. The situation neatly presaged the legal overload that would begin almost exactly a century later, in the latter years of the twentieth century.

Requests were made by the 1890s local legal profession for a law court in the city's business section near Portage Avenue and Main Street, where most of their offices were located. This idea was rejected, however, and the lawyers continued to make street car trips from downtown to Broadway at a cost of twenty-five tickets to the dollar.

Lawyer Archer Martin complained about the continuing problem of "frosty air soaring up their trouser legs" when an addition to the Broadway court house, much larger than the original, was completed in 1894. With tentative proposals that it become a three-unit complex at some future date, he could see the province was intent on remaining at the Broadway site.

About 1910, in tandem with plans for a new Legislative Building on part of the fifty-acre (twenty-hectare) Hudson's Bay Company land reserved for public construction, discussions began on the possibility of building yet another Law Courts Building bordering Kennedy Street.

This time, government policy mandated that all new buildings use only fire-resistant materials and employ every new construction technique currently planned for the new Canadian Northern Railway station on Main Street, and the Hotel Fort Garry nearby on Broadway. Materials had to be "home grown", except when not available in Canada.

Among the Made in Canada products used was a foundation of natural Portland cement made at Babcock, Manitoba, even though the Babcock operation was American owned.

The same beige Tyndall stone being used in the Legislative Building then under construction was selected for the building's exterior. It was deemed to be "of even and uniform color, free from sprawl holes, seams, sand holes, fossils and other defects".

Inside were Missisisquoi marble floors and hallways, quarried in Quebec, and walls panelled with marble to a height of nine meters. The men's lavatory has been acknowledged by jurists and lawyers as worthy of note for its marble installation, which covers all walls and floors. The acoustical resonance from all that marble became lawyer Harvey Pollack's rehearsal room prior to his victory in the world musical whistling championship.

The building was further adorned with red oak wainscotting, borders, dividers and doors, as well as brass face plates and door knobs, each custom-cast and bearing symbols of bison, wheat sheaves or the scales of justice. These remain today in the court house. So do

The judicial centrepiece of "one of the finest provincial complexes in Canada", as it appeared about 1920.

The Land Titles Building, which now serves as offices and robing rooms for Manitoba judges.

the custom-made exterior bronze main entry doors, which were purchased after World War I.

On the third floor, the magnificent Great Library was created in a traditional design with a gallery around three sides housing 100,000 books on shelves from the floor to an arched ceiling. When the room was built, the ceiling was dominated by stained glass inserts, but these were replaced with honey-combed plastic after rain seeped down on the polished study tables below.

The twenty-four-metre long assize court with its red oak panelled walls and columns, its prisoner's dock and raised judge's bench is reminiscent of court room scenes from British television dramas. There is a suitable calm and dignified silence in the marble hallways as lawyers and their handcuffed clients, accompanied by police, wend their way to court hearings.

Not surprisingly, given all this, soon after construction began in 1914, the $100,000 projected cost of this seat of the Superior Court in Manitoba, with its imposing courtrooms and accommodation for the Manitoba Law Society, ballooned to a million dollars.

Today the 1916 Law Courts building encompasses much of the history of the law in the province. It has seen it all since the days its doors on Kennedy Street first swung open. Every criminal trial, including those of the leaders of the 1919 Winnipeg General Strike, has taken place within its walls. Many of those have been the subject of avid speculation on the part of the public and, particularly in the first half-century when hanging was a possible outcome, heinous crimes were followed with a kind of horrified fascination. The trials of a serial killer, a child abuser, a bank robber and a mentally challenged farmhand charged with murder gripped the attention of men and women across the province between World War I and July 14th, 1976, when the death sentence was abolished in Canada.

In the 1980s, in a major expansion, the so-called "new Law Courts" building, was added to the complex northeast of the old building along Kennedy Street. It is the main centre for the Provincial Court of Manitoba, with courtrooms and judges' offices, and also houses registry and clerical offices. Architecturally, it integrates well with the 1916 building, but artistically it created a certain amount of controversy. Among the art pieces chosen was a stainless steel sculpture of Justice created by Gordon Reeve, professor of Fine Arts at the University of Manitoba. Stationary, with three movable ribs, the sculpture represents the stability and flexibility of the law. Other pieces by Manitoba artists in the building include bronze door handles by Eva Stubbs, cast resin hangings over the main foyer by Tony Tascona, an epoxy and fibreglass fountain by Wayne Brueckner and sixteen glass courtroom panels by Warren Carther.

When the 1916 Law Courts first opened, prisoners were brought to the court room from their cells in the Vaughan Street Jail by a private passage, allowing no contact with the public. Today, a detention centre across Kennedy Street at York expedites the transfer of prisoners to the Provincial Court.

In the beginning, the courts were entirely a male domain. Though women had been allowed to study and practice law in Ontario from 1893, Melrose Sissons' application for admission to the Manitoba Law School in 1911 was rejected on the grounds that the word "person" used in the Law Society Act did not include a woman. It took an amendment to the act, allowing her to train in the law firm of Taylor and Colwill, before she was permitted to study. However, when Sissons and Winnifred M. Wilton, (who became a law student a year later) were called to the bar in 1915, all doubts about the ability of female lawyers were put to rest, for Wilton won first prize in the final examinations. Her successors have repeated the feat many times since and today, law classes are often half female.

In the area of dress, however, tradition rules in the Law Courts. Queen's Counsel judges in Manitoba wear violet robes with mauve elbow-length cuffs and a crimson sash that hangs from the shoulder across the chest and back. Court of Appeal judges wear a shiny black silk gown that rests on the shoulders and is open at the front. Underneath are gray striped trousers or skirts and a vest edged with black buttons. Barristers wear black gowns with white tabs at the neckline when in court.

The style of the robes reflect their ecclesiastical origin. Though clerics were forbidden to plead in court 700 years ago, with lay judges and lay lawyers taking their place, the design of the robes has remained unaltered.

Judges in English courts wear wigs, but Canadian courtrooms are much warmer and the habit was abandoned. And while rulers of England provided material for official court garments, judges now purchase their robes at their own expense.

Broadway Today

The view down the boulevard today. The venerable elms have survived much over the past century, including flooding, drought and invasions of insects.

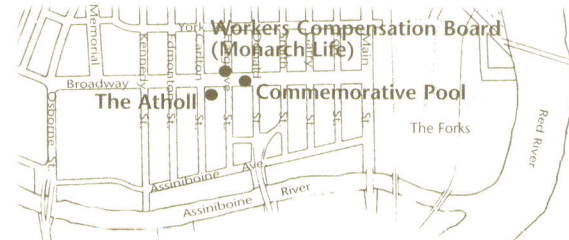

Donald A. Smith, governor and later chief commissioner of the Hudson's Bay Company, would be amazed to see Broadway today. Though his company's dreams of a luxury residential community, à la Montreal's Westmount or Vancouver's Shaughnessy, have come and gone, the business activity on the boulevard would have stirred his blood. He was, after all, a hard-nosed businessman.

Broadway today buzzes with business. Along its length are insurance, banking, real estate, legal and engineering firms as well as government offices. Scattered along the boulevard, the buildings in which they're located range greatly in age. Some, such as the Atholl Apartments, which today contains two fine restaurants as well as office space,

Broadway Today

are nearly a century old. Others, including the Monarch Life Building, now home to the Workers Compensation Board, are exemplary examples of the architecture of the post-war period.

Designed by Jim Donahue, an avant-garde professor of architecture at the University of Manitoba, and Smith

Broadway, as seen from Union Station, is a bustling place night and day, year round.

Street of Dreams: The Story of Broadway

This shimmering fountain was created in 1970 to mark the anniversary of the April 6th, 1919 opening of the Shoal Lake Aquaduct, which supplies Winnipeg with drinking water.

Carter Searle Associates of Winnipeg, the Monarch Life Building drew praise as "one of [Winnipeg's] best public buildings" in an April 1965 article in *The Winnipeg Tribune*.

"It is one of the most expensive office buildings in the city," wrote Theodore Matoff, noting that "plush economics is not the reason for its success … [rather] the functional and aesthetic aspects of the design are unified in form and space throughout."

A week later, Matoff, an associate professor of architecture at the U of M, enlarged on his view of Broadway in a second article: "The visitor forms a mental image of the city, not from its buildings but from the character of the streets. Broadway ranges from 19th Century eclecticism (for example the CNR hotel) to the contemporary technological expression [exemplified by] Monarch Life. Further, the street is assured of a consistent character through its landscaping.

"Without trees, the grouping of a few prestigious buildings along the street would be insufficient to give a humanistic scale to Broadway."

Fortunately, the trees still arch overhead today. Wiser heads prevailed during the post-war period when it was suggested that the trees be chopped

Broadway Today

down to, as Joni Mitchell wrote, "put up a parking lot". In the summer, the century-old elms create Gothic arches of greenery; in winter, the ice- and snow-covered branches glisten under Manitoba's sunny skies. Year round, the trees twinkle with thousands of white lights, a legacy of Winnipeg's first female mayor, Susan Thompson.

As the twenty-first century begins, new buildings continue to rise along the boulevard, giving the venerable avenue a throbbing modernism that bodes well for the future. And as those who work along the street will attest, Broadway is a "happening" place to be. In any season it's a great spot for dining. Between April and October, the street is filled at midday with hundreds of people lunching out-of-doors. Hot dog and falafel stands are a late twentieth-century tradition and draw crowds every noon hour as the broad boulevard is transformed into a blocks-long picnic park. For breakfast on the run or snacks anytime, a series of fast food outlets dot the avenue and in the evening, Broadway offers elegant dining at one of several fine restaurants or, for members, at the Manitoba Club.

The boulevard's also great for strolling. With its mix of Edwardian and contemporary buildings, as well

Lunchtime crowds fill the boulevard on sunny days between May and October.

as its many public institutions and heritage sites, Broadway is a fascinating place to while away a free afternoon. Its proximity to the Assiniboine River, with its summertime river walk and winter skating and walking paths, makes it ideal for a weekend jaunt.

And getting there is both easy and picturesque. In addition to being close to Winnipeg's main business section and downtown shops, malls and hotels, Broadway is a skip and a jump from The Forks, easily the most popular public place in the city. With the new Broadway Bridge, accessing St. Boniface and its fascinating francophone culture, is a breeze.

In the summer, boat buses zip back and forth along both the Red and Assiniboine, providing access to the area that is both charming and practical. In winter, the river walkways are crowded with people, particularly on weekends when tens of thousands take the opportunity to combine exercise with an unconventional view of the city.

There's entertainment on Broadway too. Winnipeg might justifiably claim to be Canada's Festival City and some of its many summer activities occur here. For example Memorial Park, a successor to Old Driving Park where the University of Manitoba buildings once stood, is filled in late June with food kiosks as a Taste of Manitoba offers citizens an opportunity to sample the cuisine of dozens of cultural entities that make up the population of this magnificently multicultural city.

And the future? As Winnipeggers are once again drawn to urban living, it might include renovating the Princeton, creating condominiums in what was once perhaps the most beautiful apartment building in the city. Whether that happens or not, Winnipeggers should get out and enjoy Broadway, Western Canada's oldest boulevard.

Further Reading

Castles of the North: Canada's Grand Hotels, edited by Barbara Chisholm, Lynx Inc., Toronto, 2000

Early Buildings in Winnipeg, Manuscript Report Series No 389, Vol. 3, Parks Canada, 1977

From Rural Parkland to Urban Centre: One Hundred Years of Growth at the University of Manitoba – 1877 to 1977, University of Manitoba, Hyperion Press

Gateway to the West: Manitoba 125 series, Vol. 3, Great Plains, Winnipeg, 1994

On the Hill: A People's Guide to Canada's Parliament, by Heather Robertson: McClelland & Stewart Inc. Toronto, 1992

One University: A History of the University of Manitoba – 1877 – 1952, by W.L. Morton, McClelland & Stewart, Toronto, 1958

Railway Stations of Manitoba, Manitoba Culture and Recreation, Winnipeg, 1984

Rupert's Land to Riel, Manitoba 125 series, Vol. 2, Great Plains, Winnipeg, 1993

Substantial Justice: Law and Lawyers 1670 - 1970, by Dale and Lee Gibson, Pequis Publishers, Winnipeg, 1973

Symbol in Stone: The Art and Politics of a Public Building, by Marilyn Baker: Hyperion Press, Winnipeg, 1986

Winnipeg: An Illustrated History, by Alan Artibise: James Lorimer and the National Museums of Canada, Toronto, 1977

Winnipeg Union Station, Kate MacFarlane and Shannon Ricketts: Historic Sites and Monuments Board of Canada Railway Station Report, Architectural History Branch, Ottawa, February 1989

Marjorie Gillies was born in Winnipeg and graduated with an Arts degree from the University of Manitoba. A food and consumer problem columnist at the *Winnipeg Tribune*, she wrote feature articles for the *Ottawa Citizen* on homes, food and senior's affairs. She has four adult children and eight grandchildren and likes searching out little known facts about people and places in Manitoba.

Heartland's Books...

Heartland's publications are portals to North America's vibrant history and natural landscapes. Our route-oriented guides appeal not only to armchair enthusiasts, but also to those who love to explore the continent's wild and historic places.

Our books are thoroughly researched, accessibly written and lavishly illustrated with rare archival images, superb photographs and commissioned artwork. We invest in high production values because we are committed to telling the stories of North America to large numbers of people.

Young Heroes of North America Vol. 1
Blackships / Thanadelthur

This is the first of a series of books by award-winning author Rick Book about real teens whose lives and actions changed the course of history in North America. Each book has two stories, both extensively researched and richly illustrated with historically accurate paintings and beautiful photographs. Aimed at young readers aged 10 and up, they bring our history to life. Each story is accompanied by a running sidebar glossary of unfamiliar words and pronunciations and Volume 1 can be purchased with one of the stories on audio CD.

color throughout
audio CD $22.95, $26.95 with CD
ISBN: 1–896150–12–8

Mistehay Sakahegan/The Great Lake
The Beauty and the Treachery of Lake Winnipeg

Winner of the 2000 Margaret McWilliams prize for popular history, this beautiful book by Frances Russell begins with the geology of Manitoba and traces its fascinating history through the lives and legends of its people.

color throughout 176 pages $24.95
ISBN: 1–896150–10–1

Exploring the Fur Trade Routes of North America

Named Best Illustrated Book in Manitoba for 2000, this national bestseller follows the fur trade from east to west along the continent's waterways. From Quebec in 1530 to Oregon in 1860, this remarkable route-oriented guide traces the history of North America through the fur trade, featuring stunning photographs, dozens of maps and full driving directions to 100 sites. An expanded edition is due out early in 2002.

full-color 256 pages $24.95
ISBN: 1–896150–04–7

In Search of Ancient Alberta

There are few places on Earth where the past is more evident than Alberta, where the plains meet the mountains. Featuring dozens of sites, more than 350 color photographs and superb paintings, this beautiful guide brings the province's geology, palaeontology and archaeology to life. Chosen by the Alberta Heritage Foundation as a companion book to its Alberta Past to Present Digitization Project.

full-color 7x10" $24.95
ISBN: 1–896150–00–4

Pelicans to Polar Bears
Watching Wildlife in Manitoba

Winner of Manitoba's Best Illustrated Book award for 1999, this Canadian bestseller includes 100 locations across Manitoba, with more than 300 rivetting color photographs, exquisite design and maps for every site.

full-color 256 pages $9.95
ISBN: 1–896150–02–0